REAL MONEY
FROM
VIRTUAL REALITY

ENTREPRENEUR EDITION

by Bob Cooney

Limits of Liability and Disclaimer of Warranty

The author and publisher shall not be liable for your misuse of this material. This book is strictly for informational and educational purposes. If you burn yourself using it as kindling in the fireplace, or any other unauthorized use, that's on you.

Warning – Disclaimer

The purpose of this book is to educate and entertain. The author and/or publisher do not guarantee that anyone will actually by educated or entertained, other than the author himself, who was thoroughly entertained. If you follow these techniques, suggestions, tips, ideas, or strategies, they may or may not lead to success. Do you really think for $25 you're going to get the keys to success? For that the author highly recommends attending one of his workshops, which has no such disclaimer. Though maybe it should. The author and/or publisher shall have neither liability nor responsibility to anyone with respect to any loss or damage caused, or alleged to be caused, directly or indirectly, by the information contained in this book. So there.

ISBN: 978-1-7329325-0-0

www.bobcooney.com

For Tim Ruse, co-founder and CEO of Zero Latency, who lured me to Australia and back into the VR industry after having one foot in my VW bus and another on a banana peel, looking to ride off into the sunset. Without his trust and vision there is no way in hell I would be writing this book. Thanks brother.

TABLE OF CONTENTS

Table of Contents

FOREWORD

UNDERTAKING A BOOK for the first time is a daunting challenge, especially for someone easily distracted. And who isn't these days? We've created more ways to distract ourselves than at any time in history. From casual games like Words With Friends to Facebook, Instagram, and Twitter, to constant notifications on our cell phones, there's seemingly no end to the distractions we allow into our lives. My antidote to this was to isolate myself, and write the bulk of this book on cruises in Alaska and the Caribbean. I booked last-minute cruises on a discount website of the same name; an inside cabin because I wasn't going for a luxury vacation.

I set out to write a book on virtual reality. For nearly 30 years I've been an entrepreneur in the location-based entertainment industry. And over that time, VR has been a recurring theme. It wasn't intentional; I didn't set out to create VR companies. But it just kept appearing in my life and having a significant impact on the trajectory of my career. I intended to write about VR, and its impact on location-based entertainment. But as I kept writing, sharing with you what I share with my mentoring clients, I realized it was becoming a marketing book.

I went through some uncomfortable processing of that concept. I didn't want to write a marketing book. There are millions of marketing books out there, and I don't feel like I have anything to add to them. I guess we all suffer from imposter syndrome at times. As I reflected on writing a marketing book, I realized that what I hate about marketing is its inauthenticity. Col Fink, one of the instructors in the Thought Leaders Business School in which I am enrolled, recently drew a distinction between "good" marketing and "bad" marketing (those are my terms, not his). Good marketing is when you are trying to influence people from a place of caring, love, and compassion. Bad marketing is when you are trying to manipulate people into doing something that's purely in your best interest. My intention is clearly to help you launch your VR product into the stratosphere, and do it in a way that is authentic, honest and "above the line."

The content in this book is designed to help you connect with the audience that needs your product. The exercises within help you get to "know" your customer. Based on my experience, and my deeper beliefs, if you follow these exercises, your market won't even know you're marketing to them. They will feel like you're reading their minds, and are offering them something from a place of caring about their needs.

The information (if you want to call it that) in this book is mostly my opinion, unless it is attributed to a third party. This is not a research paper; it's the culmination of 30 years of experience in the location-based entertainment industry. I've done my best to research what is a fast-moving industry for facts, but ultimately I am responsible for the accuracy or lack thereof. Do your own research, always.

I've tried to extract what, for me, is like breathing and turn it into an instruction manual for companies launching products in the LBVR market. If someone asked you to write a book about breathing, you might struggle. The things I do with go-to-market strategy development are based on almost 40 years of entrepreneurial experience. They've become second nature. It's entirely possible that

I've missed huge chunks of content that should be in here. It's also possible this instruction manual is complete folly, and that someone without a solid marketing background will struggle doing this themselves. Even in that case, going through the exercises in this book will increase the chances of success dramatically, however "imperfect" the exercise may be.

And now for that self-indulgent thing authors call acknowledgments.

ACKNOWLEDGMENTS

Foremost, I would like to thank my ex-wife Sharon for her unwavering support during our 25-year marriage. I would not be where I am or who I am without her.

My mom, Sondra Marino, who attends all my webinars, even though she has no idea what I'm talking about most of the time, and is my number-one fan (but not in that creepy Kathy Bates way).

Bill Bauerle, my first mentor, even though we didn't use that term back in those days.

Harold Skripsky, who saved my life in a river in Colorado gold panning, and whose trust and vision helped put Laser Storm on the map.

Chad Watkins, my first employee at Laser Storm, who even to this day comes to my rescue when I need batteries driven across the country for a product launch.

Michael Getlan, who gave me the Gipper speech when my booth collapsed at IAAPA in 1993 and kept me from throwing in the towel when Laser Storm was at a critical juncture.

Ed Bonis, my founding partner at Laser Storm, who stuck with me through thick and thin, even when he felt shafted.

Eric Schwartzman, who taught me a lot of what I know about marketing, and everything I know about PR.

Matt Church and Pete Cook from the Thought Leaders Business School, who have enabled me to fulfill a dream I truly never thought possible – write a book.

Paul Young and Lisa O'Neil, my TLBS mentors, who have encouraged me to be more than I think I am.

My VR mentoring clients, who have trusted me with their businesses, and allowed me to prove out the effectiveness of the content of this book: Tim, Scott, Kyel and Boris from Zero Latency; Leif from Hologate; Tarrnie and Kirsten from Blueprint Reality; Michael, Sylvain and Vander from Minority Media; Yuri, George and Alex from Neurogaming; Emmanuel, Julien and Olivier from Scale-1 Portal, Jonny; Barbara, Florian, and Stephen from Holodeck; Stephen, Monica, Toni and the entire team and Raydon; Jan at Virtuix; and Yoni, Ari and Ilya from Exit Reality.

Eddie, Key and Casey at Replay for giving me a forum for my musings, and convincing me my writing will find an audience.

And last but not least, I thank the universe for bringing me into the path of Kylie Savage, who not only introduced me to the Thought Leaders Business School, but who has also been a coach, mentor, and lover during much of my recent journey. She has taught me how to ask better questions, and how to hold space so people can answer them honestly and authentically. She's also exposed me to the world of human-centered design, from which many exercises in this book stem.

SECTION ONE – BEING VIRTUAL

WHAT IS REALITY? That's a big question discussed and debated by philosophers for thousands of years. Most people will agree that whatever your definition of reality, it is highly colored by your past experiences. One person might look at a sunset and feel a romantic urge to snuggle up to their partner. Another could look at the same sunset and feel a sense of time slipping away, and a desperate desire to heed a call to adventure. A third could just wake from a long day of sleep and getting ready to head to a swing shift in a factory, dreading another day in a meaningless job. So what is reality if three people can see the same thing and take away entirely different meaning from it?

Some people think we can create our own reality. Others believe our reality is predestined by a higher power, or fate. Some people believe there are multiple realities, and with practice, you can move between them. There are as many definitions, ideas, and concepts about reality as there are religions, maybe more.

Then there's the question of what is real? If I can touch it, or hear it, or smell it, does that make it real? If I can't, is it not real? What about our dreams? We see them, and feel them. Does that make them real?

Reality is worth pondering because, soon, a technology will be upon us that will make us question what is real and what isn't. We will question things we see, hear, touch, smell, and maybe even taste. Did that happen? Was it a dream? Or was it virtual reality?

The word virtual means "almost or nearly as described, but not completely." So virtual reality is *almost* reality. Now, those who have experienced VR today might scoff at that notion. Compared to our current "reality," VR is low resolution, nowhere near lifelike, and often devoid of the feedback of touch, smell, and taste. I think nobody would look at VR today and think it's "almost reality."

Virtual reality is at worst a misnomer, at best an aspirational moniker. For now, that is.

The Briefcase Phone

Those at work on the technical underpinnings of VR will tell you that it's coming. They're working hard on making VR a reality. It will take some time, but it might happen sooner than you think.

Qualcomm, the company that makes many of the computer chips that go into cell phones and VR headsets, reminded us in a keynote at the 2017 VRLA conference that we are at day one of VR. They put up a chart representing the evolution of the cell phone. The first image was a briefcase phone. Remember those? Bill Bauerle, the first consultant I ever hired, carried one. I thought he was the coolest dude on the planet. He was like James Bond.

That's where VR is today – the briefcase phone. The only people buying VR now are early adopters, tech nerds, and business people investing in the future. It's this latter group this book will focus on.

> That's where VR is today – the briefcase phone.

Sometime after I met Bill (the guy with the briefcase phone), Motorola came out with the legendary brick phone, a moniker arising from the shape and weight of the device itself. Looking somewhat like a Vietnam-era army radio, the brick was the business status symbol of the late 1980s.

It seemed like only a short time later that the Star-Tac burst on the scene, and we all had our *Star Trek* communicator. This "flip phone" was like science fiction come true. Flying cars and jetpacks couldn't be far behind! Then came the mini-brick, the Nokia 8000 series. These phones were tiny, like a baby bird in the palm of your hand. And they were nearly indestructible. I dropped mine so often that I eventually stopped worrying about it because it always kept working (except for the few times I was texting in the bathroom and dropped it in the toilet; it would be a while before waterproof phones hit the market).

The Blackberry craze brought portable email to the party, creating a whole mass of Pavlovian-responsive workers who jumped every time they received an email. Some people probably still suffer PTSD from constantly being buzzed to check in with work every couple of minutes.

Smartphones were next, but initially they weren't that smart. They offered a terrible web browsing experience, a terrible music listening experience, and a mediocre email experience. This was until 2007, when the iPhone burst on the market and changed everything.

From the suitcase phone to the first iPhone was about 15 years. Think about that. We went from a phone in a suitcase to a computer in our pocket in less than two decades. I tell this story because it's important to remember where we are in the VR world. It's still the suitcase phone.

The Law of Accelerating Returns

The pace of technological innovation we are experiencing is astounding. And it's accelerating. Futurist Ray Kurzweil claims that technological change happens exponentially. We will see 20,000 years of "progress" in the 21st century compared to the last 100 years. What took 15 years at the turn of

> We will see 20,000 years of "progress" in the 21st century.

the most recent century will probably take only 5 years now. The internet is accelerating the pace of innovation dramatically. Before the web, it took a while for people to learn about others' innovations. Now the minute they happen, they're available for the world to see and read about via YouTube, podcasts, blogs, and any manner of digital media. Before the product even sees the light of day, others are working on improving it.

VR is already changing people's lives. Wounded and traumatized soldiers are being healed, depression is being treated, families are being reconnected, workers in dangerous trades are being trained more safely and effectively, saving lives. And it's still the briefcase phone.

I've been working with VR since the early '90s. I've seen it struggle to become a mainstream technology since before I met Bill Bauerle with the briefcase phone. But the technology has finally caught up with the vision of what VR can do, and real money from big companies is pouring into research and development to make VR a reality this time.

In the next decade, like the smartphone before it, virtual reality, and its cousin augmented reality, will become the next big computing platform. It's guaranteed. Take it to the bank. Just like Nicholas Negroponte, author of *Being Digital* (the seminal book on the digital age), saw that the move from atoms to bits would transform how we do everything, from consuming media and paying for services to valuing information, VR will have an even more profound impact on society, because it will change the way we think about reality itself.

Disruption is Coming

In the near future, you'll be able to travel to Paris to view the *Mona Lisa* at The Louvre and get closer in VR than you could ever get if you flew there and fought the crowds. And it will be just as high definition as if you were standing in front of her. You'll be able to watch glaciers calving in Alaska, hear the thunderous crack of the ice, and even feel the vibration of the ground in your bones. You'll be able to attend a conference in Dubai and step up to the microphone and grill the presenter on his poorly constructed theory without risking imprisonment for your contrary views. You'll be able to sit with your ailing grandparents, listening to and recording the stories of their youth, which you can then share with your grandchildren, and with generations to come.

You'll console your daughter as she tells you of her first heartbreak from halfway around the world, putting your hand on her shoulder, which she'll feel.

Millennials, Gen Zs, and even this Baby Boomer author are exhibiting a real travel lust. Mobile technology, ubiquitous internet, and an explosion of digital jobs allows us to work from anywhere, and many are taking advantage of this by creating digital nomad lifestyles. When you can travel just about anywhere by donning a set of goggles, will you still feel the need to jump on a plane? How might virtual reality change the travel industry?

What will happen to office buildings? Companies spend enormous sums of money creating environments that foster collaboration. When we can be working in the same room together no matter where our physical bodies are located, just like we were there, is there a need for conference rooms? Is there even a need for an office? Does the boss need to stand over my shoulder and see what I am working on when he can do it by pushing a button in VR?

What about zoos? Do we need to keep animals in captivity so we can see them? Most zoos have shifted to a mission of conservation, displaying animals so we can create awareness and empathy for them, hopefully igniting a conservation movement. But when I can roam the savannah with lions and elephants in VR, why would I subject myself to the guilt of paying to see a lowland gorilla staring back at me with forlorn eyes from behind a wall of glass?

Schools, sports stadiums, concert venues, and movie theaters will all change or go away. The entire tourist attractions business will be transformed. Any place where we gather for a shared experience will become obsolete because we can get that experience without leaving our home. I am writing this book on a cruise ship in Alaska. The highlight was viewing glaciers. It cost $350 per person for 6 people to fly over the glaciers in a floatplane. What might this cost in virtual reality?

> The entire tourist attractions business will be transformed.

And if we don't need to leave our homes, what happens to the entire transportation industry? Self-driving cars are already a reality, and the sharing economy has pundits predicting the demise of the auto industry. Why own a car that just depreciates sitting in the driveway when you can summon transportation on demand? If the demand for moving from place to place diminishes, all the resources used for supporting the transportation of people become redundant. Cars, buses, trains, airplanes, gas stations, auto mechanics, tire stores – the list goes on.

This won't happen overnight. It will take decades, maybe generations, before the full impact is felt. But some industries will feel it sooner. Location-based entertainment markets are already feeling the pain of the shift towards millennial values. This might be why location-based entertainment venues have been among the first to adopt virtual reality – they see it coming.

The Uncanny Valley

It might be hard to imagine this massive shift now because the technology is so cumbersome. Bulky headsets, uncomfortable haptic suits, limited tracking technology, and low-resolution graphics all contribute to something called the uncanny valley. When a computer-generated figure displays near-identical resemblance to a human, it arouses a sense of discomfort in the viewer. This comes from the translation of a Japanese term *bukimi no tani*, coined by the roboticist Masahiro Moti, who created a graph plotting the change in the emotional response of a human to a robot as that robot's appearance becomes more human. The uncanny valley represents the significant dip in the graph at the point where the robot's resemblance to a human is perceived to be almost exact.

If you want to experience it for yourself, go watch videos of Sophia, the AI robot, on You-Tube.

> I have seen grown men reduced to sobbing on the ground after a 10-minute VR experience because it felt so real.

But even these early, barely believable experiences have an incredible impact. I have seen grown men reduced to sobbing on the ground after a 10-minute VR experience because it felt so real. What happens when we get across that uncanny valley, and the experience looks and feels so real we question reality itself?

Don't believe it can happen? Think about video game graphics. We've gone from vector graphics to photo-realistic 3D environments in four decades. And we aren't done. There are already 8K VR headsets coming to the consumer market this year. 32K will be standard within 10 years. You won't be able to see the difference between what's real and what's virtual. A few years ago, rapper Tupac Shakur reappeared from the dead as a hologram on the main stage at Coachella in front of 100,000 people. And a young, computer-generated Carrie Fisher reprised her role as Princess Leia at the end of *Star Wars: Rogue One*. Epic Games, the company famous for many innovations in the gaming industry, showcased a *Star Wars* video called "Reflection" at the 2018 Game Developer Conference that looks like it was filmed, but instead was rendered in real time on computers. It took amazing computing power, but so did *Pong* when I was a kid.

Moving Around

While graphic quality will inevitably sort itself out on a standard trajectory of improvement like we've seen for decades, locomotion is one limitation of today's VR that will take more creativity to solve. Moving around in VR is a real hassle. Try to use a joystick to "walk" like you would in a video game and nausea ensues. Teleportation (pointing at a spot and clicking to transport there "instantly") is a temporary workaround that can break immersion. VR treadmills are awkward and expensive. There are currently neural-sensing devices that can sense your brain activity. A few years ago I made a digital painting just by thinking. Soon you will be able to think about moving in VR and you will. Brain–computer interfaces will enable you to seamlessly explore virtual spaces just as naturally as you walk about the mall today. You won't need the treadmill from *Ready Player One* – which, by the way, is available today for a mere $100K.

The Other Senses

We've already witnessed great improvements in spatial audio. Our ears, being placed strategically on opposite sides of our head, do an amazing job of determining where a sound is coming from. Right now I can hear the basketball bouncing on the deck of the cruise ship behind me. I know the Latin beats are coming from the stage below me and to the left. Gaming companies have been working on simulating this for years. I remember playing *Silent Hill* on a surround sound system in my living room, by myself at night, and having to turn off the game because the sounds coming from behind me were creeping me out. Advances in headphones that simulate 3D audio are accelerating, and it won't be long before true spatial audio is part of every VR experience.

> Manhattan in the Ghostbusters VR experience, when players cross the streams at the end they're treated to the scent of toasted marshmallows.

Visuals will be hyper-realistic and audio will be spatial, but what about touch? Haptic technology is one of the more immature aspects of VR. But there are already haptic suits, gloves, and even ultrasonic haptic fields that can mimic touch. Sensors get smaller every year, and the Internet of Things, or IoT, is connecting them all together into smart networks. Wearable technology is one of the hottest tech trends on the planet. Apple's Taptic Engine chip in their Apple Watch is just the tip of the iceberg. Clothes with embedded sensors and feedback devices are easily within reach, if not in the next decade, then shortly thereafter. Sight, sound, touch; all that's left is taste and smell. The VOID unleashed the Stay Puft Marshmallow Man on Manhattan in the *Ghostbusters* VR experience, and when players cross the streams at the end ("Egon, you said crossing the streams was bad?!") they're treated to the scent of toasted marshmallows. Check.

Virtual Food?

In fifteen years we will be able to sit on the couch and go anywhere we want, with anyone who wants to go with us, and do almost anything we want. Except eat. That still will require going to a restaurant...

Having said that, even restaurants are now getting into VR. At the Hard Rock Hotel in Ibiza, Spain, chef Paco Roncero has created an immersive dining experience that incorporates both virtual reality and augmented reality. For a mere $2000 per person, guests at Sublimotion dine on Michelin-quality meals presented in a room where projection mapping technology changes the room to anything from an underwater scene to a jetliner streaking across the sky, while augmented and virtual reality bring the food to life. As the technology becomes more accessible and affordable, expect to see more restaurant implementations that transform dining from a pure culinary experience into one that stimulates all the senses.

Food and all the infrastructure needed to support it – like farms and ranches to grow it, trucks and trains to transport it, grocery stores to sell it, and restaurants that prepare it – are probably safe from VR disruption. Dining out will be one of the few things left that brings us together in the physical world, and could see a boom period.

Or maybe not. Brain–computer interfaces could eventually trick our brains into thinking we are tasting medium-rare prime rib when we're actually eating rehydrated soylent green delivered by an Amazon.com drone.

The advent of brain–computer interfaces could eventually trick our brains into thinking we are tasting medium-rare prime rib.

Digital Wardrobes

While we will still need clothes when we go out to dine, we

won't need as many since much of our attire will be virtual. In our future, the entire fashion industry could become virtual. There will be no more sweatshops pumping out imitation fashion. Instead of rows and rows of workers in front of sewing machines, there will be rows and rows of programmers creating digital versions of the latest fashion trends, which will change daily instead of seasonally.

There's already a trend towards smaller dwellings, and the younger generations are skewing towards minimalism. If we spend all our time in virtual worlds, the surroundings in which our bodies dwell become less important. Our closets will be smaller, our big screen TVs will be recycled (hopefully), and our living rooms will include some sort of chair/suspension device, or whatever we come up with that will make our virtual adventures more comfortable and realistic.

The Vortex of Immersion

The depth of our immersion in VR is, among other things, a function of the time we spend in the virtual world. The longer we stay, the deeper we go. And the deeper we go, the longer we will want to stay. It's like a vortex into Alice's Wonderland. Even with today's sub-realistic experiences, the line between fantasy and reality can blur within minutes.

> The depth of our immersion in VR is, among other things, a function of the time we spend in the virtual world.

If we wind up spending most of our time in VR, working and playing, at what point does that become our reality? Or, more important, at what point will we stop caring?

VR will connect us with people and places in ways we can only imagine. It also stands to fracture our psyches and help to create entirely false identities that could change the path of human evolution.

Facebook and Instagram have enabled people to create facades of their real lives. People offer glimpses, featuring only the highlight reel, to portray the life they wish they were living. These false realities can lead to feelings of depression among viewers, because for most people "real life" sucks compared to what they see from their "friends" on social media.

Anyone playing in the online dating arena has either been, or knows someone who has been, "catfished" – lured into a relationship with someone based on a false persona. Virtual reality will give us the tools to create entirely new personas. We can present ourselves however we want, and it will be believable – maybe even sustainable. We can finally be the person we always wanted to be. But what will be the psychological impact over time? Will we lose the sense of who we really are?

Which brings us back to the question of reality. Who are we, really? Do we have a unique soul that yearns to be satisfied? Jung suggested that when we don't live a life that is in concert with our soul's desires, we develop complexes. What would happen if an entire society just immersed themselves in an artificial reality, pretending to be what they aren't, but what they desired to be?

Some people would suggest that's what we do now. So what would change?

SECTION TWO – THE CASE FOR LOCATION-BASED VR

WHILE IT'S FUN to debate how VR will impact us in the future, more pressing for many in the VR industry today is how they can create a business that is sustainable during the emerging stages of the industry. Not everyone has the foresight of Palmer Luckey, who in 2012 launched what would become the most successful crowdfunding event in Kickstarter's short history.

The Birth of Modern VR

Oculus Rift was the proverbial butterfly flapping its wings across the ocean to create the third wave of VR. Luckey, then still a teenager, realized that the core technology needed to create a virtual reality headset was being utilized in today's smartphones.

> Oculus Rift was the proverbial butterfly flapping its wings across the ocean to create the third wave of VR.

The introduction and mass popularity of the iPhone created a category of devices that contain all the components a VR headset needs. High-resolution but small LCD screens you could wear on your face were the most visible components. Inertial measurement units (IMUs) that measure the movement of the device for applications like compass, GPS, and games were a more hidden piece of the puzzle. High-speed processors capable of rendering 3D stereoscopic images were now a norm, thanks to the explosion of mobile gaming.

Luckey built a prototype and launched it to the world to raise money for production. His Kickstarter caught the attention of John Carmack from ID Software, who demoed an early Oculus Rift headset running the video game DOOM during his keynote at the Game Developers Conference. The wave had momentum.

The $2.4 million he raised from almost 10,000 backers went towards building the DK1, the first Oculus Rift developer's kit, sowing the market with the seeds of innovation. Soon startups all over the world were showing off their virtual reality applications. From real estate pre-visualization, where you could walk through the apartment even before the first shovel broke ground, to early versions of 360-degree videos, and even first-person shooters where you were literally inside the game, if it was possible to show in VR, people were doing it. Even if it didn't make business sense.

Enter the Giants

With VR looking like a real thing, large consumer technology companies got interested. One of these was Facebook, which by early 2014 was practically printing money and had a market valuation of more than $150 billion. Facebook had been late to the mobile game in its transition to becoming the dominant social media platform, and founder Mark Zuckerberg was determined not to make the same mistake twice. So he purchased Oculus for $2.1 billion in a massive bet that virtual reality would be the next big computing platform. Facebook would be there early in the next transition, even if it was 10 years or more away.

When Oculus shipped their first consumer version in 2016, the price caught the entire market by surprise. With the first developer kit headsets priced at only $300 during the Kickstarter, the market expectation was that the final price would be somewhere in that ballpark. The announcement that the headset would cost almost $600 created a bit of panic in the market. Combined with the high-end PC needed to run a stereoscopic virtual reality game, consumers were looking at almost $2000, which was four times the price of a Playstation or Xbox One console. A high price would surely slow consumer adoption, which would limit the opportunity for application developers hoping for an iPhone App Store-like opportunity to sell their games, movies, and other applications to millions of consumers.

Perhaps sensing that Oculus would miss the opportunity to hit the mass market, Samsung jumped into the VR fray, creating a VR headset based on the Oculus reference design. Samsung Gear VR reduced the price of entry for a VR headset to under $200 for anyone who owned a Galaxy phone, of which there were over 70 million sold in 2016 alone.

While Palmer was pitching his Oculus on Kickstarter, HTC, the mobile phone company, and Valve, the uber-successful video game developer, were each working on their own VR technology. HTC was designing a headset that, unlike the Samsung version, didn't require a smartphone, but contained everything in one unit. Valve was working on room-scale tracking technology. The two companies got together in 2014 and began their collaboration on the Vive. In doing this, HTC and Valve staked their claim as the creators of *the* VR product for gamers. The room-scale tracking technology enabled a much wider range of experiences.

Now, I'm not sure who had which idea first, or who followed whom, and frankly it doesn't matter to anyone except those involved in the stories. What matters is that more than $10 billion has been invested in VR start-ups over the last few years

> More than $10 billion has been invested in VR startups over the last few years in the US alone.

in the US alone. All of this investment placed a bet on VR becoming the next big consumer product. With the infrastructure of the industry in the hands of large consumer-technology companies, I can understand the thinking. A lot of hope was factored into this expectation, but little understanding of the real history of the video game business.

What's the Problem?

For a consumer product to gain mass adoption, it needs to be inexpensive relative to the problem it is solving. VR came out of the chute expensive compared to other gaming and computing platforms. And it solved no clear problem. Sales numbers reflected this.

While the early lack of sales volume didn't seem to worry Oculus – with the cash-generating engine of Facebook behind them and who were taking a long view of VR – they needed to goose the sales engine. They introduced the first of several price drops in the summer of 2017, which eventually triggered a price war with HTC, and they now have both the original systems priced at about half their launch prices. While the price drop might have made the product look more affordable on the surface, from a consumer perspective the headset and tracking hardware comprised only a fraction of what was needed to create a VR set-up.

Besides the VR headset and tracking cameras, you need a high-end gaming PC, which costs at least $2000. This puts a high-quality virtual reality gaming rig in the realm of $3000, almost 10 times the price of an Xbox or Playstation.

This is squarely in Rolex territory. Imagine if $10 billion in capital was invested in companies building apps for Rolex wearers. Seems like a small addressable market for that level of investment.

This pricing theory masks the real problem: VR still doesn't seem to solve a consumer problem. While fanboys and enthusiasts bristle at this, it's still not clear what deep consumer need VR is fulfilling. The benefit of VR is its immer-

> "Real life: it's super immersive, has haptics that can kill you, and is ultra-high resolution."
> ~ Brent Bushnell

siveness, but are people walking around saying, "I really want to be more immersed"? Brent Bushnell, co-founder of Two Bit Circus, addressed this during his keynote presentation at the inaugural VR Arcade Summit: "Real life: it's super immersive, has haptics that can kill you, and is ultra-high resolution."

So the question becomes, what can you do in VR that you can't do in our current reality?

Why VR Hasn't Taken Off – Yet

Playing games seems to be the obvious choice to demonstrate the value of VR. But isn't playing games actually good in this reality? It's affordable, convenient, and comfortable. How does virtual reality stack up today? We've already covered the affordability part. What about convenience?

VR is about as convenient as a kitchen remodel. For an HTC Vive set-up in your living room, you need to mount cameras securely to the wall, or on stands that extend over 8' high. Then you need to move all the furniture, because when you're in VR, you can't see your physical surroundings. You need a 10' x 10' space clear of any obstructions. And you'd better lock up the dog, cat, and any small children that might wander underfoot while you're isolated in the virtual environment. You don't want to step on Fluffy, or worse, trip over her and fall, hitting your head on the coffee table that was slid just out of reach.

Xbox Kinect had a similar problem. When it launched as a $99 peripheral for the Xbox console, it was the fastest selling consumer electronics product in history, shipping 8 million units in the first 60 days. It was also built into Microsoft's third-generation gaming console, the Xbox One. Despite Microsoft investing millions in games for the platform, and encouraging third-party developers to do the same, it could not overcome the inconvenience factor, and was officially killed as a consumer product in October 2017.

A product manager for Microsoft commented on the death of Kinect, highlighting it suffered from three fatal problems.

1. It required a lot of space. People didn't want to rearrange the furniture each time they played. Consumers like being able to plop down on the couch with a controller and just play.

2. There were not enough great games. Despite selling tens of millions of units, companies didn't want to develop for it because of the awkward control mechanics and the fact that people didn't want to play on it. "Halo doesn't need Kinect," said a Microsoft insider. In addition, the best developers had invested tons of effort getting their biggest games to work perfectly with the known controller schemes.

3. It was 85% awesome and 15% frustrating. VR in its current state is more like 50% awesome and 50% frustrating. Even experts can struggle keeping the various systems working together, and constant recalibration is necessary.

Sound familiar? VR is less convenient than one of the highest profile failures in the history of gaming hardware. Awesome.

Is VR the Next 3DTV?

We now know that VR is expensive and inconvenient. So what about comfort? It's not fair to compare VR to the feeling of sitting on the couch with a controller, but factor in potential motion sickness, fogging lenses, discomfort for people who wear glasses, and the one-size-doesn't-fit-all nature of headsets that are still too darn heavy, and you need a pretty compelling reason to subject yourself to hours in VR.

But the worst part is the awkwardness. Playing VR in the living room just feels weird. You have no idea what anyone else is doing or saying, and they have no idea what you're seeing. It's just awkward for everyone.

> Playing VR in the living room just feels weird.

3DTV had a compelling value proposition when it launched. However, because people had to wear special glasses to view the picture, combined with the fact that 7% of viewers complained of headaches watching it, this was enough to derail an affordable consumer device that had the support and investment of every major consumer TV manufacturer and media company on the planet.

Is it any wonder why VR hasn't caught on yet? What I wonder is why nobody else saw this coming…

I'm not saying that VR technology won't become widely popular at some point. In the first section I pointed out how I believe it will have an impact beyond what most people can imagine. I'm just pointing out that the go-to-market strategy for the entire VR industry was fucked from the beginning.

A more informed strategy might have been to focus on location-based entertainment first, to introduce these new experiences to the masses. Video games started in arcades, and 3D started in theaters. These technologies were expensive at first, but more important, you had to experience them for yourself. They used to talk about how you can't describe TV on the radio. Can you image trying to explain a video game to someone who has never seen one? Some things you just need to try before you get it.

> A more informed strategy might have been to focus on location-based entertainment first, as a means to introduce these new experiences to the masses.

It only makes sense that VR gains its legs in the out-of-home market.

The Emergence of VR Arcades

Some industrious entrepreneurs saw this opportunity and built arcades using HTC Vive. In China, 10,000 popped up in a matter of 18 months, mimicking the wildly popular internet cafés that became a cultural phenomenon there in the 1990s. Many of these have since closed because no real profitable business model emerged. There are hundreds in the US, and at least that many in Europe. Most are run by hobbyists and VR enthusiasts with little experience of running retail entertainment establishments. Business models are still questionable, and it remains to be seen how they pan out.

The traditional amusement market has been slower to adopt VR. They see the limited throughput, high relative cost, hygiene issues, and fragile consumer hardware as significant concerns. A few companies have been able to transcend these problems by developing commercial-grade solutions, and coming up with turnkey platforms that make the consumer experience so compelling that operators will overlook the inherent limitations.

Now that the consumer market has dropped into what's called the "trough of disillusionment" – that point where an overhyped technology fails to meet the expectations of the market, and everyone turns their attention to the next thing (Google the Gartner Hype Cycle for more) – the larger VR industry is looking at the location-based sector and pivotting their strategies.

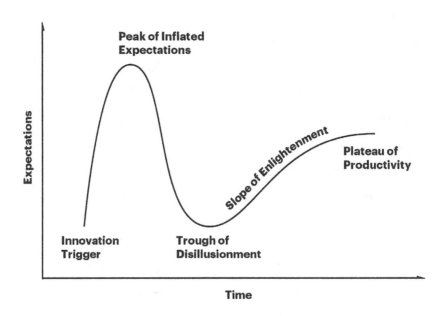

HTC saw the opportunity presented by location-based VR early. In November 2016 they unveiled Viveport Arcade, a commercial B2B version of their consumer app store for VR games and experiences. Viveport Arcade encourages developers to opt-in for commercial use, and VR arcade operators can download games they can legally offer to the public. HTC collects a revenue share and pays upstream to the app developers.

It was a smart business strategy for HTC, because in the words of Viveport's president, they were struggling with awareness. "One of the big problems we have is a marketing problem for virtual reality, and this is a way to get the Vive out there before VR is ready for mainstream home adoption," Rikard Steiber told *The Verge* in November 2016.

Think about that for a minute: he wants entrepreneurs to open VR arcades so they can help him market a product that when people buy it, they'll no longer need to go to the arcade. It's brilliant and evil simultaneously.

> Viveport's president, Rikard Steiber, "One of the big problems we have is a marketing problem for virtual reality."

Video arcade operators saw this story play out in the 1980s and it didn't end well for them. The consumer games market eroded the video arcade market until what was left was unrecognizable. HTC's strategy would have been more nefarious if it weren't so transparent. If VR only suffers from a marketing problem, operators ought to be storming the HTC castle with pitchforks and torches. But the problem goes deeper than marketing and awareness, as I have explained.

Where's the Killer Game?

Brent Bushnell, speaking on LBVR at VRLA this year, said that VR still needs its great game – the game that will sell the hardware: "Let's face it – the console is a tax on the game. Nobody bought Xbox; they bought *Halo* and paid the console tax." The same can be said about *Legend of Zelda* and *Super Mario Brothers* for Nintendo, and *Final Fantasy* and *Metal Gear Solid* for Playstation.

> Brent Bushnell, "The console is a tax on the game. Nobody bought Xbox; they bought Halo and paid the console tax."

The problem is that developers are frequently hedging their bets on VR by releasing titles across 2D and 3D platforms. Lucky Tale, developer of the game *Star Child* for the PS4, made their game work in both VR and on flat screens. Same for *Resident Evil*, which had the chance to be the console seller, but Capcom wasn't willing to make that bet. Maybe soon we will see more companies like Survios go all-in with VR. We're more likely to see that happen with the new wave of all-in-one headsets like Oculus Quest, coming in 2019, as the "console tax" on a loaded HTC Vive rig is still north of a couple grand. When the tax gets down into the hundreds, and the experience can meet people's expectations, hopefully developers will place bigger bets. Until that happens, we're unlikely to see mass consumer adoption, unless a small startup creates the killer game that is worth the headset tax.

Meanwhile, location-based entertainment operators will see the benefit of billions of dollars of investment being targeted towards their business. Developers are converting their games to be more arcade friendly, and new companies are entering the market with quality turn-key attractions featuring virtual reality. If you're one of these intrepid entrepreneurs who are bringing the future of VR to the location-based market, I encourage you to read on.

SECTION THREE –
SUCCESSFULLY
LAUNCHING YOUR
VR PRODUCT

THIS NEXT SECTION will walk you through the details of my 13-week program to launch a VR product into the location-based entertainment market. I've run this program with great success with many companies. Most of the exercises and theories contained here are what I would consider basic marketing tactics, and are the building blocks of a solid go-to-market strategy. I hold no illusion that there's magic in here, and any experienced marketer might look at the words on these pages and say, "Tell me something I don't know." This book is not for you.

In my nearly 40 years of working in startups, I've come to realize that many of my fellow entrepreneurs are not marketers. They're inventors, salespeople, leaders, story-tellers, engineers, scientists, hustlers, or combinations of the above. But rarely are they marketing experts. This section is for them.

The objective of this program is to find and describe the unique value of your product. If you're like most entre-preneurs, you love your product, and understand its value deep in your gut. You've been thinking about it for a long time. You've been living, sleeping, eating, and breath-ing it. And you probably think that if you just put it out there, people will beat a path to your door. That's called the "better mousetrap fallacy," a mistaken notion that if a company pro-duces a product technically better than its competitors it will be more successful in the marketplace.

The reality is, nobody else cares about your product.

I'm here to burst that bubble for you. Nobody else cares about your product. It's just one of a million other prod-ucts out there trying to capture the attention of consum-ers. The sooner you grasp this concept, the better off you will be. I know dozens of entrepreneurs who build amazing products, yet were astonished when people didn't line up to buy them.

If you launch a product without uncovering and then positioning its unique value, you risk leaving piles of money on the table in lost sales, lost margin, or both. You might have gotten away with this in 2015, when VR was just emerging and almost anything virtual would garner immediate media attention, resulting in lots of "free" publicity – but not today.

In 2017, the whole VR market finally woke up and realized that the consumer appetite for VR had been overestimated. Everyone with a VR product, seemingly all at once, looked at location-based entertainment as their salvation. Hence the market is getting crowded. Dozens of VR products entered the location-based market this year, with even more coming next year. If you don't develop a unique value proposition targeted towards a specific market segment, through which you unlock tremendous value for your customers, you will be left to compete on price, which becomes a race to zero.

I run this program as a mentoring workshop with early-stage companies that already have products or, at a minimum, solid prototypes. This section can act as a guide to engage your team in the process of understanding the needs of various market segments and uncovering the unique value of your product, so you can dominate the markets you enter. This will lead to maximum sales velocity and increased profitability, so you can reinvest and grow your market dominance.

Profit is the fuel for your company. If you don't earn a solid profit, you can't reinvest in your product roadmap, your people, your positioning, or your business. At best you will

> **Profit is the fuel for your company.**

be creating a job for yourself, and for most entrepreneurs that's not why they take the risk and put forth the Sisyphean effort. I can't promise this formula will lead to profits – there are way too many variables in starting a business for that. I can promise, however, that if you follow this program you will increase your odds dramatically.

What is a Go-to-Market Strategy?

My definition of a go-to-market strategy is a plan that considers a company's strengths and resources, and uses them to match the unique value proposition of the company's product or service to the specific needs of a market segment, so the company gains a competitive advantage and can sustain a profitable business.

Let's unpack this.

Strengths and resources – Every company has its own unique strengths and resources. It might be a patented technology, a large cash war chest, a solid reputation, a great team, etc. Finding your unique strengths, not only of your product, but also of your company, can uncover opportunities to position your product against your competition so it really resonates with your potential customers.

Unique value proposition – If there's one thing I believe is the most important part of this process, it's finding and describing your unique value proposition in terms that your market will understand. It's what makes your product different from all the other products in the market, and what will hopefully enable you to not compete on price. If you're selling a product that is undifferentiated, you will need to use very different sales and marketing tactics than if you're selling a highly differentiated product. Light bulbs are a great example of this. When was the last time you bought a light bulb? Did price factor into your consideration? What about brand? Once you decide if you want incandescent, LED, or fluorescent, your choices come down to brand and price. If you're a startup, you have no brand awareness, so you're left to compete on price. Don't be that company.

Market segment – Too many startups try to be all things to all people. When you do that you inevitably become nothing to anybody. If you want to succeed, you need to narrow your market to a segment that needs the value your product delivers. I know this runs counter to what many venture capitalists will tell you, and I understand that sometimes you need to show a large addressable market to make money. That's why your investor presentation should not be your marketing plan. But when you narrow your market, you can become known as the market leader relatively quickly.

> If you want to be successful, you need to narrow your market to a segment that really needs the value your product delivers.

You can easily get to know the needs of your customers, and then you become known as the company that understands them. This will lead to a market-dominant position where you can dictate price, and maintain solid margins so you can reinvest in growth. Don't worry, you'll still attract business from other segments, and once you dominate one segment you can move into new segments, dominating them, too.

Competitive advantage – Ultimately, if you're going to run a profitable company you want to find a sustainable competitive advantage. This is becoming more and more difficult in an age where technology is super accessible and copycats are everywhere. It's especially hard in the location-based VR space, towards which it seems every other company is pivoting. You can still succeed if your competitive advantage isn't sustainable, you just need to make sure you re-run this process continually to keep a keen eye on how your competition is positioning their products, and be nimble in your own positioning.

Profitable business – No matter why you started your company, the scorecard we should all use in our business is profit. Sales growth is nice, but at the expense of profits requires capital that is hard to come by in the location-based VR industry. Venture capitalists are looking for companies that can scale fast and big, and location-based anything is more like a bricks-and-mortar business, which scales slowly. Employee growth can feel good, but all you're doing is increasing your overhead. Profit enables real growth, reinvestment in product to build new competitive advantages, and can be used to reward employees so you feel good, too.

So how do you create a go-to-market strategy that will lead to rapid growth and a profitable business? It's going to take some time and concerted effort by your team. It's work, but without it you're relying on sheer luck or fortune to get where you want to go. When I run this process with a client, depending on how focused they want to be, I can usually facilitate a great result in two full days, plus a month of weekly follow-up calls. Give yourself a full calendar quarter to run this whole process, as you'll be learning on the fly and having to do some basic research I typically bring to the table in the form of decades of experience.

The Kick-Off

The go-to-market strategy process is best run as a group

exercise. Bring together as many stakeholders as you can. You will want to include your key employees, representing engineering, marketing, sales, executive, finance, and whatever other functions you have in the business. Often in a small startup these roles are shared, and that's OK. I've done this with small teams of 2–3 people, and large teams of more than a dozen. It's important to have a diverse group representing not only different functions, but also different ways of thinking. Diversity of thought is a key to innovation. Do not do this in a room by yourself.

Carnegie Mellon University's Entertainment Technology Center conducted a four-year study that showed expertise diversity dramatically increased innovation. More diverse teams led to more conflict, which led to more innovative work. Conflict can also disrupt a culture and any process, so we will spend some time talking about how to manage conflict in a productive manner.

One way to limit destructive conflict is to make sure everyone's expectations are aligned at the beginning, and throughout the process. The best tool I know for that is the expectation map, which allows everyone to voice their expectations regarding the process, participation, and outcomes.

Tips and Tools

I will be recommending basic tools to use during the exercises in this section. This is by no means the only way to do it, just how I've found works for me. Use them, discard them, change them, or whatever suits your style.

Try to find a room you can use for the entire process, one with plenty of wall space. It's important that you have access to the room and can keep your notes on the wall for the duration of the project. Nothing is more disruptive than having to continually move your stuff from room to room. Natural light is good, because you'll be spending lots of time in this room in the next quarter. You can also use the windows for sticky notes!

You will want a whiteboard; a mobile one is ideal but not necessary. A whiteboard is perfect for illustrating big ideas, like ecosystems.

I use a lot of sticky notes. Buy them in multiple colors and sizes. In fact, buy all the colors and sizes. And only get 3M Post-it Notes, the extra-sticky version if you can find them. The off-brand notes tend to fall off, and when you're in a project space with hundreds of notes falling to the ground like leaves in an autumn windstorm, you will curse yourself for not heeding this advice.

The colors can identify different groups or themes in the exercises. Different sizes will be used for exercises of different scope. Some exercises are done with one person on an A5 sheet of paper, so smaller notes make sense. Others are done on a whiteboard or wall, and you want to write big enough to see from across the room.

When you write on a note, use a sharpie and write in ALL CAPITAL LETTERS (sorry if you thought I was shouting). This will enable everyone to read the note. This is harder than it looks, as we've been taught to not write in caps. You might need to enforce this rule in a draconian fashion in the early stages, but it will pay off in the end.

Use one idea or concept per note. Try not to write detail, because you won't be able to read it. Encapsulate the idea in a title on the note, and then explain, encouraging people to ask questions to gain clarity and a shared understanding.

A sticky note used as a title or to name a cluster of ideas should be placed at a 45-degree angle so it looks like a diamond. This helps differentiate content from context/concept.

Another sticky note trick is that when you peel the note off the pad with the adhesive at the top, peel from one side to the other, NOT from the bottom to the top. This will prevent that curling that makes notes fall from the wall. #mindblown

Speaking of walls, unless you have a cavernous room with unlimited wall space, you will want to move groups of stickies occasionally. This is where butcher's paper comes in. You can usually find it at an office supply store (you can also use brown packaging paper). Make sure it's not glossy, and test the adhesion of the sticky notes to the paper before buying it. When you run an exercise – let's say competitive segmentation – you will eventually have all your competitors in neat little groupings on the wall. When it's time to move on to the next exercise, you're going to want to move the segmentation work to the side, but still in view. If you use butcher's paper, it's easy – just move the paper. If you stuck the notes on the wall, you'll spend the next 15 minutes moving and rearranging all the notes individually. Then the next day you'll find half of them on the floor because moving them reduced their stickiness.

The best way to get butcher's paper to stick to the wall is

with blue tack, or some other gum-like adhesive. You can find this at office supply stores as well. It comes in little dots, or sometimes in perforated blocks. It's like chewing gum that's been chewed already, and works like a charm.

You might be tempted to use those large 3M self-adhesive flip chart pads, but Post-it Notes don't stick well to them. You'd think 3M would have figured that out, but no.

Throughout this section I will also refer to templates I use, like Empathy and Expectation Maps, Segmentation Workbooks, SWOT Analysis, etc. You can download examples and templates for these on my website: www.bobcooney.com/tools

Many exercises will require a facilitator. The facilitator's job is to ensure full participation, to keep things moving and on subject, and to ensure the co-creation of outcomes. If you use an insider to facilitate, try to select someone who is a

It might not be the best idea to have the CEO facilitate as the leader's personality could dominate the process.

good listener, and has the respect of the room. It might not be the best idea to have the CEO facilitate as the leader's personality could dominate the process, and I can tell you from personal experience that while the CEO might think they're approachable (I did), employees are typically on guard with their boss in the room.

Here are some basic facilitation tips:

> There are no bad ideas.

- **There are no bad ideas.** Don't shut down an idea because you disagree with it. This could cause others to hesitate to offer an idea that could unlock something valuable to the process.

- **Remind the group that the expectation is to stay focused.** Don't be afraid to re-focus the group if they wander down a rat-hole. However, before you interrupt, make sure it's a rat-hole and not an exploration that could lead to something valuable.

- **If something is valuable but out of sequence, it's OK to park it for later.** Create a parking lot for things you want to address at a future time, even if it's after the session. This will allow the people holding onto that idea to move on.

- **Try to let the group decide when there is ongoing debate.** Look for consensus and buy-in. If it looks like that's not going to happen, is there an expert in the room you can defer to?

- **Use probing questions to stimulate productive and inquisitive conversation.** Use open-ended questions instead of binary (yes/no) questions. Invite debate and disagreement.

- **Encourage participation.** If someone is disengaged, try to involve them.

There are great resources for facilitators on the International Association of Facilitators website at www.sessionlab.com/library/iafmethods. You can also find professional facilitators in your area, or you can always contact me.

Expectation Maps

Once you identify your core team, bring them into a room for a kick-off meeting. Set the context of the project for them. Explain what a go-to-market strategy is, and why it's important to the success of the company. (If you're not clear on this, go back to the previous chapter and read it again.)

You'll want one copy of the expectation map for each person, and plenty of sticky notes and sharpies. You'll be asking each person to reflect on what they want out of this process, and to write each exception on an individual sticky note, placing it in one of the four segments of the map.

The expectation map has four segments: See, Hear, Say/Do, and Think/Feel. The four segments engage the different parts of participants' brains. Most people experience things using one or two parts. Forcing people to use all the aspects of their brain will achieve a more well-rounded result.

> Forcing people to use all the different aspects of their brain will achieve a more well-rounded result.

Which segment they actually place their expectations in is almost irrelevant. Often the same expectation can go in multiple places, so don't let your contributors fret over that. It's just a thinking framework.

See – What do you want to see at the end of the project?

Hear – What do you want to hear at the end of the project?

Say/Do – What do you want to be saying or doing at the end of the project?

Think/Feel – What do you want to be thinking or feeling at the end of the project?

I often like to give an example of a completed expectation map, but within an entirely different context so as not to lead them to an answer. Here is an example:

Expectation Map for an Amazing Surf Session:

See: Chest-High Waves / Dolphins Playing / Empty Line-Up / No Closeouts

Hear: Crack of a Cold Beer Can Opening

Say/Do: Catch and Ride 10 Waves

Think/Feel: Relaxed / Tired / Present / Grateful

Again, where they place their expectations on the map is not important, and point this out repeatedly. Often people will get stuck on not knowing where to put things and it can paralyze them. This is an individual exercise that requires quiet reflection. I usually allow about 15 minutes to complete the first phase.

Once everyone has identified their expectations and placed them on their map, it's time to share. Each person is encouraged to come up and place their expectations on a shared expectation map on the wall, explaining what it means to them. Encourage questions to make sure that everyone has a shared understanding of each person's expectations. Go around the room until everyone is done. If you're leading the exercise, you might want to go last to make sure you don't influence the group.

Once everyone has gone, ask the group what expectations they heard that surprised them. You might allow people to add any expectations that came up for them during the exercise. At this point you can cluster the expectations by theme.

I often find that people's expectations fall into categories and can be similar to one another. It's helpful to look at these expectations and ask the question, "What's this about?" Clustering everyone's expectations like this can help you keep track and make sure you're meeting as many as possible throughout the process.

Going back to my surf expectation map as an example:

Expectations	What's it About?
Chest-High Waves, No Closeouts	Wave Quality
Relaxed, Grateful, Present	Mindset
Empty Line-Up Catch and Ride 10 Waves	Not Being Hassled
Cold Beer	Celebration

Once you've clustered the expectations by theme, have someone document the results and post them publicly where the team can see them. Check in throughout the process to see how the team feels about the progress you're making vs. their expectations. There are many schools of thought on how often to use this exercise. I use it to align expectations of the entire project, and then check in every week or two. You can also use this at the beginning of each major section of the project, i.e., positioning, distribution, and launch plan.

Don't get too caught up in the process. It's just a framework for having thoughtful dialogue around expectations.

You can't do it wrong. As long as people feel free and safe to express their expectations, and you're all listening with the inten to understand, you'll find this is a valuable exercise that will help solidify the desired outcomes of your team.

Positioning
The Competition
Since positioning is an exercise in relativity to your competition, you need to understand how your competitors position their products. There are several exercises you can use to get a solid handle on your competitive landscape.

Competitive Landscape
The first thing you should do is take to the internet. While you might think you know your competitors, sometimes spending time on Google can show you companies you didn't even think of. You might also want to use Incognito or Private Search in your browser to eliminate Google's propensity to show local results.

Start with searching by the terms you use to describe your business. Let's say you're making a free-roam VR system. You might want to search for:

- Free-roam virtual reality
- Warehouse-scale virtual reality
- Multiplayer virtual reality
- Virtual reality arena, etc.

Each search will yield additional results. You also might want to broaden your search to News, expanding the time scale by clicking on Tools.

Click through each result that looks relevant and build a spreadsheet listing all the competitive products you find, and paste the URL into a cell for each product. (This is a project you can give a researcher on Fiverr if you don't want to spend the time doing the searching yourself.) Go broad, the broader the better. Even if the results are barely relevant, you can always narrow your focus later.

Once you have a solid list of competitive products in the leftmost column of your spreadsheet, it's time to bring the group together to review their websites. Ideally a projector or large monitor works best. You can also divide and conquer, giving each team member a certain number to research and then report back to the group. If you have a lot of competition this could be a more efficient method.

First sort your competitors, with the ones you believe to pose the biggest threat to your business at the top. Trust your gut on this, you know who they are. They're the ones you lay awake at night thinking about. Starting with the website of the company at the top of your list, look at how they're positioning their product. Some questions you might want to ask (feel free to come up with others):

- What do they charge?
- How many players can play at once?
- How much space does their solution require?
- Do they project revenue for their customers?
- How many employees does their solution require to operate?
- Who is their target market (age, income, gamer, hardcore, etc.)?
- How many titles do they offer?
- How long have they been in business?
- How many locations are they operating in?
- Who are their distributors?
- How do people buy their product?
- How much equipment do they provide?
- Is there redundancy of equipment (spares, etc.)?
- What is their support program?
- Where are they located?

Each question should be at the top of a column in the spreadsheet, and the answer for each company will populate a cell at the intersection of the company/product and question. As you review more companies, you will notice that products are positioned differently, and more questions might pop up. Specifically note the top five things that each company seems to call out as their main features and benefits. This will enable you to see openings in the market where you could differentiate.

The next thing you need to do, if you haven't already, is to try out the top competitive products. This will enable you to identify their weaknesses, since these most likely won't be

It's often hard to admit to yourself what a competitor does well.

listed on their website. Have as many people as you can go through them, writing up detailed reports with an eye towards their strengths and weaknesses. Try to be mindful of your bias towards focusing on their weaknesses. It's often hard to admit to yourself what a competitor does well.

Add the key strengths and weaknesses to your competitive landscape document, then it's time to do some segmentation.

Competitive Segmentation

Now it's time to group your competitors into segments. Segmentation enables you to make sense of the competitive landscape, especially as it gets more and more crowded. Looking at a competitive list of dozens of companies can be overwhelming, making it impossible to see where the cracks are for you to create your differentiated positioning.

Segmentation takes a bit of creativity. There are no hard and fast rules. How you segment the competition is highly dependent on how you view the market and how you view your product.

A high-level segmentation might look like this:

- Multi-Player Turnkey Arcade Solutions (Hologate, Chaos Jump from Minority Media)

- Single-Player Turnkey Arcade Solutions (WePlayVR from AISolve, X-Cube from Exit Reality)

- VR Arcade Software Management Solutions (Springboard VR, Private Label VR, Synthesis VR)

- Free-Roam VR Solutions (Zero Latency, Sandbox VR, The VOID, Nomadic)

You can go on and on, and get really granular. The more granular, the better. For example, you could take Free-Roam VR Solutions above and break it down further:

- Free-Roam Co-Op Games (Zero Latency, Symosity)

- Free-Roam Competitive PvP (MassVR, Ventus VR)

- Free-Roam with Environmental Haptics (The VOID, Nomadic, Dreamscape)

- Free-Roam Experiential – Non-Gaming (TrueVR, Sandbox)

The more you segment, the more you will find companies fitting into one or more segments. That's OK.

I've found the best way to run the segmentation exercise is collaboratively, with sticky notes and sharpies. Put a sheet of butcher's paper on the wall for each segment you're tracking. Write the name of the segment on a large sticky note and place it at the top of each piece of paper at a 45-degree angle, so it looks like a diamond. Write the name of each company on a sticky note and place it on the paper with the appropriate segment. Remember to use capital letters. If a company resides in more than one segment, create multiple sticky notes for that company. This will give you a good visualization of the market.

Now you should see some patterns emerge. I can't tell you what they will be, because it's different for every company and every exercise. But by now hopefully you're seeing early signals of what segments your product might fit into, and who the key competitors will be.

Competitive Ranking

Another useful exercise I find is force-ranking the competition within the segments you're playing. I like to do this on a two-axis basis. Along the bottom of the butcher's paper, draw a horizontal line from left to right. Along the left side, draw a vertical line from bottom to top.

In a group, discuss what two things make a competitor the most threatening. Some possibilities are:

- Brand awareness
- Number of locations
- Amount of funding
- Number of distributions
- Price
- Amount of content

There are many more, but typically there are two big ones that will stick out for your team. Write one on the bottom axis, and another on the left axis. Starting with the bottom axis, take each company's sticky note and ask where along that axis you would rank them against the others. This is a forced ranking. Every company will either be to the left or the right of the other companies. There are no ties. Be diligent. You will have to move them around. A company might start at the far right, and then move towards the center as you discuss other competitors. That's normal. Once you're done you should have a line of competitors at the bottom of the chart with the most threatening on the right, the least threatening on the left.

Next consider the vertical axis. Start with the company on the far right of the horizontal axis, and ask the same question but though the lens of the new axis. How threatening is this company compared to the others? Move it up or down, but keep it in the same horizontal placement. Go through each company, moving them up and down, but not changing their side-to-side alignment.

When you're done there will be a cluster of companies towards the top and right of the graph. Circle them with a sharpie. These are your key competitors in that segment. You might also find that a company is highly ranked on one axis, but low on the other axis. These are companies I would watch, because if they're smart (and always assume your competition is smart), they are working on their weaknesses.

You can repeat this exercise for multiple segments you feel you're competing within. At the end of the exercise, these are the companies you will need to consider when we get to positioning.

SWOT Analysis

What is SWOT? SWOT is an acronym for Strengths, Weaknesses, Opportunities, and Threats. It's a well-known, tried-and-true marketing exercise that's apparently been taught in business schools since the 1970s. I wouldn't know, because I didn't go to business school.

In my early days as an entrepreneur I'm sure I rolled my eyes when some b-school grad suggested running a SWOT exercise in one of my companies. So if you're rolling your eyes now, I understand.

In my decades as an entrepreneur, mentor, and coach, I have since found this exercise clarifies the value proposition relative to your competition with which you will go to market.

- Strengths are things about your product and company that give it an advantage over others.

- Weaknesses are things that place your product or company at a disadvantage.

- Opportunities are things that your business could exploit to become an advantage.

- Threats are things in your business or the market that could undermine your success.

Strengths and weaknesses tend to be internal, while opportunities and threats tend to be external, but not always. Don't get hung up on that.

The quality of the insights that come from SWOT analysis are only as good as the work you did in the previous competitive analysis. If you don't understand your competition, the results will be inaccurate and probably useless.

> Not everyone is willing to speak up about organizational and product weaknesses in a group setting.

This exercise can prove challenging, especially around identifying the weaknesses of your own product and company. Not everyone will speak up about organizational and product weaknesses in a group setting, especially with the founder or executives in the room. If you're in an alpha-lead role you might want to step out of the room for this part, and let the rest of the team run with it. When they're done they can brief you as a group, then you can add your two cents' worth so nobody feels vulnerable when being critical.

I've often found that organizational weaknesses come up during this exercise. It can be cathartic for employees to vent their frustration about the problems they experience in the company. When this happens, I use a separate piece of butcher's paper to create an organizational page on the wall. When someone throws something out that is an organizational weakness that doesn't impact the product positioning, I park the note on the organization page and encourage the team to address it in a different meeting later.

Plan to run this exercise with each of the top competitors from the competitive ranking in the previous exercise, and then with your own product. Run all the way through the SWOT for each product, rather than looking at all the strengths of the products and then all the weaknesses. Use a different color for each competitor. (More on this later.)

I find this works best as a group exercise. Have four separate pieces of butcher's paper with the word Strengths, Weaknesses, Opportunities, or Threats at the top. Place them on the wall in a grid like this:

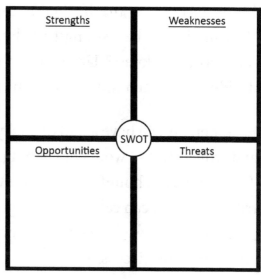

Then we will start with strengths.

Strengths

It's always easier to start with strengths. These are the things that companies tend to put forward on their websites and in their marketing materials. For your product and company it's the things you lead with when talking to your customers, prospects, and investors. It helps if you're willing and able to be honest with yourself. One person might say something is a strength, while the rest of the team might call bullshit and say it's actually a weakness. That's OK. You're looking for a shared understanding.

It's important for the facilitator to encourage enquiry. Why might this be a strength? Why might someone also see it as a weakness? Ultimately it's up to the group to decide where each thing lies on the matrix.

Each person will have a pad of sticky notes and a sharpie and will write 1–3 words describing a strength on a note. The facilitator should make sure everyone gets to contribute. People can call out a strength, then stand up and place it on the wall. Keep it to one idea at a time, and allow time for discussion.

It can be more efficient if you give people a few minutes at the start to think about their list before they write them down. Then each person can take turns posting one of their notes as you go around the room.

Once the group has exhausted their strengths, it's time to move on to weaknesses.

Weaknesses

While it's easy to find the obvious strengths of your competitors by just reviewing their websites, weaknesses are not so apparent. This is where having experience and reviewing your competitors' products will yield benefits. If nobody on the team has tried out your competitors you'll have a hard time with this exercise.

One way to suss out the weaknesses of your competitors is to find online reviews from customers. This could be on bulletin boards, Reddit, TripAdvisor, Google, Yelp, or wherever other users of their products might go to vent

One way to suss out the weaknesses of your competitors is to find online reviews from customers.

their frustration. Press coverage is another place where balanced reporting (is there still such a thing?) will usually call out the weaknesses of a product, experience, or service.

When you look at your internal weaknesses, each one can seem like an opportunity if you choose to work on turning it into a strength. If you're not disciplined you will go through an entire SWOT analysis and have nothing in the weakness section but a whole bunch of stuff showing up as opportunities. Fight this urge. This is where the internal vs. external lens can help. Strengths and weaknesses tend to be internal, and opportunities and threats external. If it's an internal thing, make it a weakness if you're in doubt.

Finding weaknesses in your own company and product requires a certain level of self-awareness. Often founders of early-stage companies ignore them to stay focused on marketing their strengths. Don't get caught up on internal weaknesses. This is a good exercise and gives your team a chance to voice their concerns and views, which can actually help you find the holes in your products. But we will work mostly with your strengths and your competitors' weaknesses.

It's worth repeating that if you're an alpha-type leader, you might want to step out of the room and give your team an opportunity to work on the internal weaknesses part themselves.

Opportunities

As I've mentioned, opportunities and threats tend to be more external. Opportunities could be environmental trends in the marketplace, mindset shifts of customers, the growth of markets, new models of doing business, general awareness growth, or a million other things. It could be a new movie coming out that you want to license, or a potential pivot to a new tangential market. Counting the number of potential opportunities for a business can be like counting the stars.

> Counting the number of potential opportunities for a business can be like counting the stars.

You want to focus on opportunities that align with your core competencies and current or near-term market opportunities, otherwise the exercise can get out of hand. Set this context up front with the group, otherwise you may find yourself shooting down ideas during the exercise, which can be de-motivating.

If you find clear differentiated positions within your strengths, you might just park the opportunities for further consideration. If you're not finding a clear differentiation opportunity within the strengths of your product and the weaknesses of others, then you may decide to prioritize one or more opportunities that prove to be key differentiators in your go-to-market strategy.

Threats

Threats are all around. If we spent our day focusing on them, we might never get out of bed in the morning. Being aware of them enables you to position against them before they become apparent to your market. Once you complete this exercise, no matter how much I try to convince you to run this process every 6 months, the odds are you won't do it again – at least not for the product you're launching today. This means that when one of the threats you identify actually looms large, you won't be adjusting your messaging to position against it. And your sales will be impacted, though you may never know why.

Threats could be nascent competitors, or changes your competition might make that undermine your unique value in the market. Often in the VR market, the threat of technology obsolescence leading to disruption is significant. An example of that happening right now is the emergence of robust inside/out tracking systems that are going to make the cost of optical tracking systems seem outrageous. If you built your solution around hundreds of thousands of dollars of optical tracking technology, you're being disrupted as I write this.

Threats can also be opportunities simultaneously. The lack of consumer awareness of VR makes marketing a challenge, but the flip side is that people don't have the tech at home, which makes location-based VR such a field of opportunity. It's perfectly OK to have one idea in more than one category.

What's It All About?

When you're done, you will ideally move the strengths of your main competitors into one consolidated competitive SWOT. Since you used a different color for each competitor (you remembered that, right?), you can take the sticky notes for each main strength and move them onto one piece of butcher's paper. Cluster all the similar strengths together. Ask the team which strengths are similar to each other.

For example, one competitor might have a large content library, a second might have large movie-IP licensed games, and another might have a few very high-quality games. If you asked "What's this about?" the answer might be "content". If they all had large libraries it might be "broad selection of content".

You need to cluster the competitive strengths around concepts like this to make sense of them. If your four key competitors all have similar strengths, you might consider that to be "table stakes," or a baseline requirement to enter the market. If your competitors have too many "table stakes" features you don't measure up to, consider a different market segment (we will get to that later) so you can compete with a different group of competitors. If your competitors are well entrenched, this can make it even more challenging. Write down the table stakes features on a separate sheet and take them off the board.

Now do the same for competitors' weaknesses. As you cluster them together, are there some common weaknesses you might exploit? Talk about them as a group.

Write each weakness you want to exploit on a separate sheet of paper and put it on the wall with blue tack.

Once you're done with your competition, it's time to go back to your product SWOT.

Go through the same exercise with your strengths. First look for strengths you possess that exist as table stakes. You can cross these out on the table stakes paper as they negate each other, and the market will assume that you offer these. An example I see all the time is fast return on investment. Everybody says that, so saying it is almost redundant.

The ones left on that sheet are things you will need to sell against until they are developed and added to the product. Your product team should add these features to the product roadmap and prioritizing them.

I know there are those who will disagree with this last statement, and there are many examples of when this would be bad advice. One example would be if your differentiated position is strong, and your approach is radically different to the competition. My guess is that if you're in that position you're not reading this book.

Now look for unique strengths you possess that your

competitors lack. Capture each of these on a separate sheet of paper. These are your competitive strengths. We will be using these to build your competitive positioning.

Now you can look at the opportunities. These could be the things that allow you to sustain your momentum in an evolving market. Are there opportunities on the board that could exploit a hole in your competitors' strengths, or maybe attack one of their shared weaknesses?

> Your competition is probably not going through this rigorous thinking. By doing this you're setting yourself apart and increasing the likelihood of success.

Up to now this exercise has been looking at your top competitors as a group, because when you create your messaging platform, you never know which competitor your prospective customer is considering. If you have a particularly well-established and dominant competitor, it can be worth doing this exercise specifically against their SWOT. You might find you need to focus your competitive positioning against a single company.

One last word on this process: your competition is probably not going through this rigorous thinking. By doing this you're setting yourself apart and increasing the likelihood of success. Don't get caught up in trying to be perfect. There is no such thing. Do the best you can. The process is as valuable as the outcomes.

Features and Benefits

Now that you've identified the unique attributes we will use to distinguish your product in the marketplace, it's time to put some language to the process. We will create a messaging platform that will enable prospective customers to connect with and understand the value of your product, and how it fits their needs and potentially solves their problems.

It's been said that people buy benefits, not features. This is because people buy products that solve problems. These problems can run the gambit from a broken refrigerator, in which case the consideration process is short, typically before the food in the freezer thaws, all the way to finding the perfect home, which can take months or even years.

Virtual reality systems can range from an almost

impulse purchase – such as the 70 systems Hologate sold at the International Association of Amusement Parks and Attractions show in Orlando in 2017 when they launched – to a year or more with a free-roam VR system that requires dedicated real estate and costs $1 million or more.

No matter the product, or the reason, the purchaser is looking to solve a problem. It could be as simple as they're bored with the current game selection in their arcade and they want a new shiny thing. Or it could be they were on the tail end of the last business trend and want to be on the leading edge of what they see as the next big thing. There's no shortage of buyer motivations, but they are never about product features. They are always about benefits.

"This product does this" is a feature statement. This is where many companies go wrong. They get caught up in the features of the product and fail to think about it from the perspective of the customer.

"It solves this problem" is a benefit statement that will address a customer problem. Ideally you want your statements to include both features and benefits.

"The Amazing VR System has the highest throughput (feature) so you can handle your busiest times and keep you customers happy (benefit)."

This may seem formulaic, and it is, because it works. It may also seem simple, but it's not easy. It requires a discipline that even long-term professional marketers struggle with.

What's In It For Me?

Another way to check if your marketing language is customer-centric is to see if it meets the WIIFM test. No, this is not the name of a radio station; it stands for "What's In It For Me?!" This question is posed from the perspective of the customer, NOT you or your organization. Most companies fall into the trap of talking about their products from their own perspective, which sends a powerful subliminal message to your customer that you don't understand or, even worse, don't care about their needs and problems.

> WIIFM stands for "What's In It For Me?!"

"Our product is the first of its kind" is a company-centric statement. I see this all the time in the VR world. World's first free-roam VR. Sydney's first VR escape room. Oma-ha's first VR arcade. Nobody gives a shit that your product is the first of its kind except you. That's a statement that serves no purpose other than to feed the ego of the company founder. It's nice that you're first, and your family and friends should be proud of your innovation. But what problem does that solve for your customer?

"You will see these benefits from these features solve these problems that you have," is a WIIFM statement from the customer's perspective. The shift is powerful. All of your marketing language should be run through the WIIFM filter. If it doesn't clearly state why it benefits the customer, it needs to be reframed or eliminated.

Writing Your Feature Benefit Statements

With your radio tuned to WIIFM, it's time to write your own feature and benefit statements. Going back to your SWOT analysis, let's start with the table stakes features as practice. One way you can out-market your competitors is to do a better job of positioning your table stakes features as feature and benefit statements tuned to WIIFM. It's likely that your competitor isn't doing a great job of this.

Take each table stakes feature and write it on a piece of

paper. What is the key feature, and how can you describe it in a way that your customer will understand?

Here are some rules:

No jargon – Your customer might not know the meaning of frame rates, latency, occlusion, or many other industry terms that get thrown around. If so, you've lost an opportunity to influence their consideration process towards buying your product. You will also do subtle damage to your credibility because you risk alienating them, by either making them feel uninformed, stupid, or that you don't understand them. Customers buy from companies they like, respect, and trust. If you talk down to your customers by using jargon you will never develop their trust.

> If you talk down to your customers by using jargon you will never develop their trust.

No abbreviations – This is like jargon. The exception I will make is VR. You don't need to type out virtual reality every time. But don't solely use VR either. Mix it up. If you talk about your frame rates you will want to not only explain what they are (see the jargon paragraph above if you forgot already), but also spell out frames per second instead of using FPS. Here's an example of using frame rate in a clear, concise, feature benefit statement:

> "90 frames of video per second gives your customers a silky smooth and believable experience that eliminates the discomfort that can sometimes lead to motion sickness."

I can't tell you how often I've read "We maintain 90 FPS" as a marketing statement. I guarantee you that most potential VR buyers out there have no idea what that means.

If it's short and clear, it will be digestible. Think tapas, not Thanksgiving turkey.

Clarify it – Nobody has time to read a novel. That's why podcasts and audiobooks are so popular now. Don't fall in love with your shit and write an essay that requires reading. If it's short and clear, it will be digestible. Think tapas, not Thanksgiving turkey.

Avoid weasel words – As much as, almost, as little as, are all weasel words. They're basically little lies hidden in copy. Be direct and honest.

Find your voice – Mark Manson wrote a global bestselling book called *The Subtle Art of Not Giving A F*ck*. It was based on a blog post he wrote with the word "fuck" in it 127 times, (for the record, I only use it 5 times in this book.) He found his voice. What's yours? I'm not saying you should litter your marketing copy with profanity. What I am saying is that you need to find your tone. It is serious? Is it light? Is it humorous? Knowing your market can help you, and if you're unsure, then somewhere in the middle of serious and light is a safe place to be. If you haven't done a real brand study yet, then this can be an important decision, because you'll be building your brand unconsciously, which can affect your company's success years down the road.

> Don't be boring. If you can't help it, find someone else to write for you.

Make it memorable – Great copy stands out because it captures the reader. Don't be boring. If you can't help it, find someone else to write for you.

Long, Short and Sharp

A really effective way to create your feature benefit copy is to write each one in long, descriptive format, short, impactful format, and then as something sharp and catchy. If you capture this in a document it can become what my friend and marketing communications expert Andre Lawless (www.lawlessmarketing.com) calls a messaging platform. You can then hand this to a designer, or any marketing person, and they can know they are staying on-message and on-brand. You will be, too.

One danger I see all the time is that company owners tire of their own stuff too fast. This can be a product feature, an entire product, a brand, a logo, or just marketing copy. When you're tempted to change something because you or your team is weary of seeing it, think about your customer. Are they tired of it? Have they even seen it yet? Most times the answer to this question is no. Just leave it be.

Most marketing campaigns can run much longer than they do. Repetition is powerful, as people need to see and hear something multiple times before it sinks in and they remember. How much of this book will you remember a week from now? Now think about all the marketing messages we're bombarded by every day. How many can anyone remember? Just because you're looking at it all the time doesn't mean your prospects are.

So, a solid documented messaging platform can work wonders for your company, product, and brand. Here's an example:

Long and descriptive – VR Product X offers the highest player density of any free-roam VR platform in the world. This means up to 20 people can play together, so you can attract large parties and corporate events, filling up your off-peak hours with high-margin revenue.

Short and impactful – With 20 players at once, VR Product X opens up the large corporate event and party market.

Sharp and punchy – No more angry moms because you had to break up Tommy's birthday party so they could all play VR four people at a time.

If you go through this process with each feature benefit statement, your marketing will be on-message and consistent no matter what form it takes. You can hand this over to your marketing communications resource and they can update your website, brochure, sales deck, trade show booth, and all the other marketing stuff you've created to date. Or you can create from scratch.

Once you're done, you will need to agree on the top 3–5 value statements that will be your leading messages. These should strongly consider your differentiated position. If you love that your product has a certain feature that is shared by many of your competitors, remember that's table stakes, and you can't lead with it and seem differentiated.

> Bad design will undermine great messaging every time.

One tip: if you don't have a good graphic designer who knows how to create marketing collateral, seek one out as they can be worth their weight in gold. I've seen more than one company go through this process to come up with great messaging, and then try to build their own sales collateral. Bad design will undermine great messaging every time. There are plenty of great designers out there. If you don't know what great design is, ask someone who does. If you think you want to do this yourself, get outside opinions from people who will tell you the truth, and check your ego at the door.

Distribution

Now that we know your product and its core value propositions, we can look at the market to determine which customers might be best matched to its value and how we get it into their hands. I call this distribution, but in a broader sense than the term might otherwise imply. The goal of this section is to create a common understanding among your team of the distributor, vendor, and operator space across multiple market segments and figure out how to maximize their impact for your product rollout.

In this section we will create an ecosystem map to determine the players and their relations to each other; use empathy maps to determine what they might actually want and how we might fulfill their business needs; consider the physical production of getting the product in the hands of your customers; plus service and support, pricing, sales and distribution, compensation, and more.

Segmentation

The first step is market segmentation. By segmentation I mean what pieces, or segments, of the market will your product most likely resonate with best?

Segmentation can often prove a challenge for entrepreneurs who see their product as perfect for everyone. While that might prove true, it's much more effective for a startup to find a smaller number of customers who will love it, where it solves a significant problem for them in ways other products don't. They will become passionate promoters of your product, and talk to people in other segments – and you can grow from there.

You can also become an expert in a small market rather quickly, building relationships, understanding problems, and becoming known by your customers as the company with the product that really "gets" them. This is powerful positioning that can help you maintain your margins in the early days, when many companies wind up discounting to grab market share.

> Become known by your customers as the company with the product that really "gets" them.

I like to do this as a group exercise, with stickies and sharpies. You'll be surprised at how many market segments a group can come up with. Ask everyone, one at a time, to call out a potential type of customer, write it down on a stickie, and post it on a whiteboard or wall. Some examples of popular segments in the LBVR space could be:

Movie theaters, theme parks, zoos, family entertainment centers, shopping malls, bowling centers, skating centers, museums, trampoline parks.

The list goes on and on. I've done this exercise with groups and had 50 segments on the board when we were done.

Once you run out of steam, group them together by some common attribute. This could be a demographic target audience, experience type, or something else that becomes apparent when viewed through the unique filter of your company and product. For example, you might group museums, zoos, and science centers together because they are primarily educational, and/ or they attract tourists. Once you have them grouped, name them so you have a language for discussion.

Now discuss if any of these groups don't seem like a natural fit for your product. Take them off the board. Are there some groups that might be a fit, but you're not sure?

Or maybe you need more product development to meet their obvious needs. For example, does a market cater to kids but your hardware is heavy? Could you reduce the weight through some engineering effort? This group can go on a back burner. Move them onto a piece of butcher's paper that has "Later" at the top.

Are there any groups where you know your product is a good fit? Where there are some obvious product–market fits? If one naturally jumps out and everyone agrees, focus on that one. But usually there are 3–5 that look intriguing. If that's the case, let's get to work on those to get a better understanding of their needs and how your product might fit them.

The tool I like to use for this is an empathy map.

Empathy Maps

An empathy map is a way to put yourself in the shoes of your customer to understand what their needs might be. It requires a certain level of self-awareness and, you guessed it, empathy. You need to suspend your judgments, biases, and assumptions to put yourself in the position of another.

For this exercise it's helpful to have at least two people

for each segment. Depending on how many segments you have, and how many on your team, you might need to run this session more than once.

Take each segment and consider the customer; usually he or she will be the owner of the venue. If you're considering selling to museums, it helps to understand who makes the buying decisions. If you're selling to large chains, you might have several people in the decision matrix.

One way to ensure you're fully considering the position is to ask these four questions through the lens of experiencing your product:

1. What does your customer want to see?
2. What does your customer want to feel?
3. What does your customer want to hear?
4. What does your customer want to say or do?

One example might be that your customer will want to say to all his operator peers that he's made his money back on your product in 6 months. Or he might want to feel a sense of joy because his customers are so happy when they experience your product.

Like the expectation map, this thinking framework makes sure you're engaging all of your senses. Most people approach the world with a primary sense. Some of us are talkers, some are feelers, some are listeners, some more visual. Thinking about the customer from each perspective will give you a more well-rounded and complete empathy map.

When you're done, you will have a picture of how your customer might view success through the lens of your product. Now, ideally you will want to discuss this with target customers in your target segments. Depending on your resources and timing, you might decide to do this at an early stage, or wait until you have a primary segment identified. It really depends on how well you know the market. I've been successful in creating pretty accurate empathy maps because I've been talking to operators for almost 30 years, and have a pretty good sense of what they're looking for. Your mileage on doing this in a vacuum may vary.

Ecosystem Map

Once you have your segments done, and your empathy maps, you can map the ecosystem. We do this to identify who is in the ecosystem and try to determine the level of complexity at play. You can have the best product with the most compelling benefits, but if you can't get it in the hands of the customer, you're fucked.

A great example of this is Tesla, who developed a direct-to-market car distribution scheme bypassing dealerships. Customers would go to a showroom in a mall, pick out the car, customize it, order it, and have it delivered to their home. However, in some states car dealerships are actually protected by legislation. As of 2018 it is still illegal in 16 of the United States for a car manufacturer to sell directly to a consumer. If you want to buy a Tesla in Texas or Connecticut, for example, you need to travel to another state. Coming up with a distribution strategy is critical.

> You can have the best product with the most compelling benefits, but if you can't get it in the hands of the customer, you're fucked.

Building an accurate and meaningful ecosystem map will take collaboration, industry knowledge, and insights.

In the VR ecosystem, there are developers, publishers, movie studios, licensing agencies, hardware suppliers, technology integrators, solution developers, streaming networks, operators, locations, distributors, etc. It's a complex ecosystem.

You can start with categories like those in the previous paragraph, with one category on each piece of butcher's paper. Or you can just start naming companies and placing each one on a whiteboard, then grouping them the way you did with the market segmentation exercise. It's a good practice to map out the entire ecosystem as best you can as opportunities might emerge in discussion you might not have seen before.

Once you have the ecosystem defined, explore the relationships within the system. Who serves whom? What is the value exchange? Are there exclusive relationships? Are they contractual or relationship based? Who might block your entry to the chosen market segments? Who can grease the skids?

Once you have mapped out the ecosystem to the best of your ability, the best practice would be to have discussions with the most important ecosystem members.

Assign team members to contact several constituents of each ecosystem component. Every team member can become an expert in their designated channel. Together you will have a well-rounded view of the ecosystem.

Once you've had these conversations, reconvene your team and create empathy maps for each ecosystem component. Draw out insights from these empathy map discussions. What are the requirements of the key ecosystem partners? What challenges and opportunities exist? How might this impact your pricing, costs, margins, timings, etc.?

Take your time to get this part right. It's going to take hard work and some real digging to get the truth, especially if you're new to the market. Some ecosystems are highly tribal, and if you're an outsider they will be wary. It might pay to bring in an industry expert to help gather some of this understanding and shortcut the process.

Distributors

Now that you have your ecosystem mapped and your team is understanding the potential distribution channel opportunities, it's time to pick a distribution method. At the highest levels, there are two ways to get your product into the market: direct and indirect. Depending on your market segment, the indirect channels can be complex. Direct might seem simple at first, but I promise it will be more complex than you expect.

One question to consider early on is – what channels does your most direct competitor use? How solid are their relationships? For example, in the coin-op amusement industry, TouchTunes, an early pioneer in the digital jukebox business, locked up distributors with a golden handcuff promise of a percentage of their recurring revenue streams from music licensing royalties. As long as the distributor maintained an exclusive distribution relationship with TouchTunes, the royalties would continue. This was a key strategic move on their part that made it difficult for new entrants in the market.

> Every industry has a distribution channel. Some are more effective than others.

Every industry has a distribution channel. Some are more effective than others. Often they can offer things that might not be apparent on the surface. You should have discussions with as many of them as possible to understand what they offer.

I recently discussed with a bank looking to do more financing of VR systems in the amusement industry. They won't finance equipment from a "vendor" that is a startup. Knowing the definition of the word "vendor," however, is critical. If a distributor is reselling the product to the operator, then they are the "vendor" in this transaction. So finding experienced distributors can provide a crucial means of financing the purchase of equipment for your customers.

Don't be fooled into thinking that if you go through a distribution channel you will not need to have a sales and marketing team. It will be smaller, but you will still need to create and drive demand. Distributors are staffed with humans. They often take the path of least resistance to success. They will go where the money is. If another product is easier to sell, or pays higher commissions, that's where their effort will be concentrated.

If your key competitor is not going through distribution, or is mostly selling direct but offering a smaller than normal commission to the distribution channel, this could present an opportunity to gobble up some market share by being generous and meeting the demands of the distributors. If the competition already has distribution locked up, then maybe you can offer a much lower price to the operator, passing along the commission to them in the form of price savings. There are no right or wrong methods, and sometimes a combination of strategies is the answer.

Many distributors have long-standing relationships with customers. If you sell direct, know that distributors who might feel spurned by you could sell against you and you would never know. Often operators consult with distributors on their purchases. Some do, some don't.

If you utilize an established distributor, make sure they're right for you and your product. What is the price range of the products they normally sell? If your product is $250K, and their average product is $20K, it might not be a fit, because the sales process of selling something for a quarter-million dollars differs from twenty thousand. What about the length of the sales cycle? Is it a match? If your sales cycle is 6 months and their typical sales cycle is 60 days, will their sales staff have the patience to continue to follow up, or will they get bored and frustrated, leaving unclosed opportunities on the table? What types of financing will they offer? Will they showcase your product in their showroom? Do they conduct open houses? Will they market with you? What about trade shows? Will they feature your product on their stand? These are just some questions to ask during your consideration process.

It can also help to talk to other companies utilizing the distributors you're considering, especially ones that are non-competitive, maybe not even in the VR space. How is their relationship with this distributor? You can learn a lot over a beer.

Software Distribution Platforms

Something that many VR software companies are struggling with is how to distribute their game to the market. There are some amazing VR experiences and games being developed, but not a lot of VR infrastructure. What do you do if you have a great game and want to sell it to location-based entertainment locations?

At the highest level there are two methods: a game distribution platform aimed at generic VR hardware in arcades and family entertainment centers (FECs); or partner with a manufacturer or infrastructure company to build dedicated hardware to feature your software experience.

On the game distribution front, one method is to utilize Steam, which is an app store designed for consumer video games but repurposed for LBVR. There are now better options. Springboard VR, Private Label VR, and Synthesis VR are three companies that have created software and content-distribution platforms for location-based VR centers. Most of their content is centered on room-scale VR set-ups utilizing HTC Vive, but they're expanding their capabilities and are worth checking out.

My problem with all these models is that they operate on a pay-per-minute model, where the consumer pays by the hour or increment thereof, and the content provider gets a percentage of that. Selling anything by the minute tends to commoditize the experience, and VR so amazes that I hate seeing the current race to zero in the marketplace.

> VR is so amazing that I hate seeing the current race to zero in the marketplace.

This pricing practice harkens back to the days of LAN gaming centers, when kids would show up to play multiplayer PC games before high-speed internet became ubiquitous.

LAN gaming centers sold time on their machines. They weren't delivering anything different to what people had at home, it was just connected so people could play competitively. It was a cottage industry of hobbyists, and they mostly went out of business. The VR arcade business feels like a repeat of this.

If you think of an arcade, most operated on credits. If you were good, you got to play longer, because you died less frequently. Driving games gave you time bonuses for hitting certain checkpoints. Nobody decided what games to play based on how long they lasted, though you might select games at which you were better to make your money go further.

Today, with debit card systems in family entertainment centers, some locations have chosen time-based purchases. This is a value-driven pricing model. They are focused on families and competing for their hard-earned money against all manner of entertainment, from movies to bowling to staying home and watching Netflix or playing Fortnite. Arcade games have been around for decades – to be honest, they're getting stale, and deserve to be discounted.

Virtual reality is brand new, it's exclusive, and it's amazing. You can't do it in many places – yet. Customer satisfaction ratings are through the roof (if you believe the Google reviews). It appeals to millennials, who are well documented to prefer spending on unique experiences rather than things.

I can't think of a single other location-based entertainment business that markets its experiences on a per-minute basis. Nobody decides which $15 movie to see based on its runtime. And theaters don't charge less for a movie that's 87 minutes than one that runs 3 hours.

> Theaters don't charge less for a movie that's 87 minutes than one that runs 3 hours.

Bowling centers charge by the game, with some exceptions for lane rentals that are time based. Escape rooms charge a flat fee per experience, and have the unique quality that if you solve the room fast, you actually have a shorter experience. But nobody complains that they solved the room in 45 mins instead of an hour and demands 25% of their money back.

For the VR arcade industry to go mainstream, they need to look at different business and pricing models.

Some companies have tried to license directly to locations. Survios (makers of Raw Data and others), VR Nerds (makers of Tower Tag), and others have gone to a per month, per computer license. This requires the operator to dedicate one station or more to the game to ensure that people are playing it to recoup their fixed monthly royalty. This is a better model, and ultimately the per-minute model will fall away.

Manufacturers/Resellers

The other option that more companies are choosing is to create a dedicated hardware platform to feature their game(s). Hologate came to me in 2017 with a reference design for a four-player truss-based system with two games that they wanted to bring to the FEC market. I introduced them to Creative Works, a laser tag arena manufacturer in the US. Creative Works founder Jeff Schilling actually managed one of my Laser Storm arenas back in the 1990s, and turned his passion for laser tag into one of the leading companies in the amusement design and build business. I thought it would be a great fit. They went on to sell more than 70 systems at their

IAAPA launch in November 2017, and have sold another 100 since then. Hologate had developed a great software platform and some entertaining VR games, and that was their core competency. Partnering with a manufacturer/reseller with a long-standing reputation in the industry was a key component of their explosive success.

Another company taking advantage of the need for physical VR infrastructure is Exit Reality in California. They started in 2016 by converting a food truck into a roaming VR exhibition, helping brands to create VR events around the country. They're now building single and multiplayer hardware systems that, when partnered with software platforms, become turnkey products, which is what much of the industry is looking for.

> They want a turnkey product that they know is being supported from both a service and future development standpoint.

The VR arcade market is dominated by VR enthusiasts who are happy to tinker with off-the-shelf parts and turn them into solutions and experiences. The more mainstream location-based entertainment market doesn't have the time, expertise, or patience for this. They want a turnkey product they know is being supported from both a service and future development standpoint.

We will probably see more companies pop up that can help software companies get their games to market. This is a new market opportunity for everyone, and the ecosystem will probably evolve rapidly.

Pricing

There are several components you need to consider when pricing your product. Competition, revenue generated, and your positioning are primary considerations. The cost involved not only in developing the solution but also in building and distributing it, including sales and distribution commissions, and your ability to meet the volume demands of the market, are also important.

Many startups take a finger-to-the-wind approach to pricing, and either leave money on the table or undercut their margins

If you underprice your product, you could create more demand than you can fill and leave a lot of money on the table.

to the point they can't operate a profitable business. If you under-price your product, you could create more demand than you can meet and leave a lot of money on the table. Conversely, if you price it too high and nobody buys, discounting can create a stench in the market that is hard to overcome.

I like to take both a bottom-up *and* top-down approach. The bottom-up approach is when you look at your internal cost model, starting with your projected cost of goods sold (COGS). This includes things like the cost of manufacturing, labor to produce the product, shipping costs of bringing in components (inbound freight), and direct labor to produce the product (but not research and development, ongoing support costs, or general overhead labor). One way to distinguish between COGS and overhead is by asking whether the cost increases proportionally with your production volume. If it costs you $100 to build it, and you build 10, will it cost you $1000? And if you build 100 will it cost you $10,000 (not counting efficiencies in purchasing at volume)? If it doesn't increase proportionally, then it's operational overhead.

Things like support costs, marketing expenses, and commissions are generally broken out separately but need to be considered as well. Your commission plans might be tiered, where a salesperson or distributor gets a different commission rate based on their volume sales.

For a low-volume product, I tell my clients to target a COGS of around 50% or more. It's inevitable you will underestimate the costs of getting your product to market and sustaining the support organization necessary to deliver quality service. There are so many hidden costs in starting a business that it's nearly impossible to accurately project them. So be conservative. If you're making too much money, you can always refund some back to your customers, right?

Distributors can demand up to 20% of retail sales prices. In some channels, distributors prefer to set the price based on their knowledge of the market. But be careful taking their advice in setting a retail price. Their leverage on a sale is much higher than yours. What I mean by that is if you make a product that costs you $50K to get out the door, and you want to make a 50% gross margin, you will price it at $100K to distribution. If they want to make 20%, they will mark it up to $125K. They might tell you that's too high, that the market will only support a $100K price point. So you agree and drop your price to $80K, so they can sell it at $100K and still make their 20%. Now you're only making $30K gross margin, which is a reduction of 40%, while the distributor is making $20K, which is a reduction of only 20%. It's often in the best interest of the distributor to keep the prices down, because it generates higher volumes and the lower price doesn't hurt them as much as it hurts you.

Once you've come up with a bottom-up price, it's a good idea to check it with a top-down model. This is typically done by looking at the competition's pricing, your test earnings, and ROI models for the operator. Many solution providers will take their revenue numbers and then divide it into their sales price and claim they offer an ROI to the operator in that many months. With VR, this can range from misleading to downright dishonest. At least for now, labor is a significant cost component of operating a VR attraction. If you require an attendant to operate a single-player VR game, your ROI will be stretched quite far if you're willing to be honest with the market.

Not every operator will staff a VR attraction in the same way. One of the early challenges for some VR attractions in the FEC market was that operators installed them thinking that people would be lining up to play. They didn't understand the need to both market the attraction outside their walls, and to sell it *inside* their walls. This means putting their best member of sales staff as the attendant for the VR game, so they can convince people to try something they don't understand. Instead, many just didn't bother staffing at all, and the systems just sat there – and they blamed the product for the failure.

It's imperative that you manage customer expectations if you want to succeed. If your solution requires a certain a level of staffing, make that known in your marketing materials, and make sure it's factored into your ROI equations, and ultimately your pricing.

Depending on the segment you're selling into, the ROI expectation of the market could range

If you can sell your product maintaining a 50% gross margin, while offering an operator a reasonable shot at a return on investment in less than a year, you have a good shot at being successful.

from 6 months to 2 years. Anything beyond 2 years is risky, because the technology is evolving so quickly. What looks like a solid investment today could be obsolete within 24 months, and if the operator hasn't gotten their money back by then they've probably made a mistake.

If you can sell your product while maintaining a 50% gross margin, while also offering an operator a reasonable shot at a return on investment in less than a year, you have a good shot at being successful.

Fear-Based Pricing Decisions

Pricing is a constant point of debate among VR operators – what will the market bear? On one hand you have The VOID getting $35 for a 12-minute VR experience. On the other you have VR arcade operators charging as little as $25 for 1 hour in a room-scale HTC Vive. And there's everything between. I've never seen such a new, expensive, and amazing technology quickly become commoditized in a race to zero. I chalk this up to a lack of sophistication and experience, and emotion-driven pricing rationale.

Zero Latency has been charging AU$88 for a 45-minute VR experience for over two years, and is running at over

90% capacity over a 7-day operating week. Octane Raceway in Phoenix is charging US$50 for 25 mins, and 60% of their players are repeat customers.

Yet I constantly hear people rationalize that their price is low because lower prices encourage repeat play. When I ask them for any data to support that, they just stare at me.

A very sophisticated operator in Latin America has been experimenting with various VR attractions. They first thought they needed to run shorter games, despite my urging that the data suggests longer games are more enjoyable, and will yield a higher ticket price and lower labor costs. They ignored the data and went with their experienced intuition. After two months they conceded that they were wrong, and now want to go to a longer game at a higher price. But they also said that it was hard because even though the data supports it, it feels risky and they're nervous. This is a company generating 9 figures in sales per year, operating in multiple countries.

So is it any wonder that entrepreneurs with little experience are dropping their prices?

When Zero Latency opened in Madrid, initial sales were slow. Alberto Marcos thought he had a pricing problem.

They had priced the initial 25-minute VR experience at 35 euros. Madrid was coming out of a recession and the unemployment rate for millennials, his target market, had only just dropped below 20%. Did he have a pricing problem, or an awareness problem?

Well, it's easier to drop your price than to increase your awareness. And when business owners open their doors and don't see the traffic and sales they projected, it's easy for panic to set in – especially if there's not enough working capital to survive a long growth curve, or enough to up their marketing spend.

Alberto dropped his prices to 25 euros, and all that happened was sales dropped. The same number of people came, but at a lower price. Then he used Groupon, which increased awareness but decreased his margins again. Not until he engaged a small, local PR firm did things turn around. Now they are looking to increase their pricing again to almost 40 euros. And sales are up 400%.

One alternative to the per-minute model is for arcades to offer dedicated experiences in each "booth". VR World in Manhattan operates this way. Patrons pay $59 for an all-day pass, and then queue up for the game they want to play next. There have been complaints about the queuing system, which is home-grown and buggy. But the concept is sound. It creates a more social space, as people aren't just diving into their booth for an hour, then leaving. They play a game, get in queue for the next one, and have conversations. They play another game, then maybe go to the bar for a drink while they're waiting for their next turn.

VR World also charges extra for premium experiences, such as their Moveo motion platform, or their *Flatliners* experience in the basement.

Operators who use the per-minute model complain that if they adopted the per-experience model they would need more booths. You can't offer all the experiences people want in just 6 or 8 rooms. VR World has over 50 computers. Maybe this is the cost of being in a sustainable VR business?

Curating a Social Experience

Part of the problem is that operators aren't focused on the entire customer experience. Back in the laser tag business, we didn't advertise a per-minute price. We advertised a per-game price. And when people asked how long it was, we didn't say it was a 10-minute game, we said it was a 20-minute experience. We included the briefing and vesting time, and the post-game scorecard experience. It was a three-act play. The briefing was the set-up; the game was the conflict; and the scorecards the resolution. It was all part of the experience.

Part of the problem is that operators aren't really focused on the entire customer experience.

What if we looked at VR the same way? I recently spent a day mentoring a prospective VR arcade operator in a small city of about 300,000 people. When she got to pricing, she said "You're going to hate me!" I knew immediately what she would say, and she already knew what my reaction would be. She told me how in her town, people didn't want to pay for indoor entertainment, so she didn't think she could get more than $30 per hour. And I said, "Maybe you just shouldn't be in this business."

She had no data at all to support her thesis. And she was trying to overcome her pricing problem by creating more things for people to do. She thought she could create a social experience by having chairs so people could hang around and watch their friends in VR. She wanted to have other things for people to do, but none of this added up to enough revenue to generate a profitable and sustainable business. It also put her at risk of someone else coming in with a higher budget and building a nicer place in a better location, or coming in and undercutting her on price. There was already rumors that another operator from a nearby city was eyeing up her town.

However, instead of trying to convince her to raise her prices, I came up with another approach. Recognizing that any good story has three acts – the Set-up, the Conflict, and the Resolution – we envisioned a new 60-minute VR arcade experience for $30 that could offer tremendous perceived value without diminishing her inventory utilization.

A player books a time, let's say 6:00pm. They show up at their allotted time to be ushered into a nice ante-chamber, where they sit on a couch with the 7 other people who have booked that slot for Act 1, the Set-up. A host comes in to brief them on what to expect, and a couple of headsets are available for people to play with, to get a feel for how they go on and how to adjust the settings. There's a few iPads so people can browse the games they might want to try. The host helps them decide which game they will play in their 30 minutes of actual game time. Hopefully some will play the same game, to make it more social. But even if they all choose different games, it creates a great shared experience when we get to Act 3.

One problem with most VR arcades is that operators don't think about the first-time user experience, or FTUE as it's called in game design. Great games offer a great FTUE. But most consumer games assume the player has hours to learn how to play, not seconds. When a player has never used VR before, it becomes

> **One of the problems with most VR arcades is that operators don't think about the first-time user experience.**

even more important. Getting some questions out of the way in a social setting makes their actual in-game time more valuable.

Once they decide on their games, the host can load them up in the appropriate station and the players are set to go into Act 2, the Conflict, where they deeply immerse themselves in their virtual reality experience. Once they vacate the ante-chamber, the next group that booked the 6:30pm slot can enter for their first act. When the 6:30 group is done playing, they move to the reflection room for Act 3, the Resolution. This is another room like the ante-chamber, where players can share their experiences. If you use a mixed reality platform that records players inside the virtual experience, like Mixcast or Liv, players can view their videos right there, sharing them in the room and, more important, on their social streams. If they played different ent games they can compare notes, and encourage each other to come back to try them next time. The host can then offer to book their next session at a discount if they commit on the spot, increasing repeat visits.

The thing about this that most excites me is that it curates a social experience.

An operation like this will run a higher labor cost. But it should yield a customer experience much better than what I've witnessed at innumerable VR arcades. It also doubles effective per-minute revenue from 50 cents to $1 per minute, by doubling the throughput. Double the customers also means double the rate of viral advertising, and increasing repeat visitation reduces marketing spend.

However, the thing about this that most excites me is that it curates a social experience. Couples can come in, sit close and just talk to each other and ignore the other players if they want. Large groups can come in and enjoy each other's company. I've witnessed complete strangers play a co-op virtual reality game then, at the end, book another session with their new friends.

We will be prototyping and testing this design, and I am sure it will need tweaking. It's just one example of how looking at the entire customer experience enables you to design something that delivers higher value and charge the price that VR, and you, deserve.

I bring all this up because consumer pricing is crucial to your product's ROI for your customer, which is critical to your

If you're not thinking about how your operators will be pricing your product to their customers, you're missing a key component to the value chain.

ability to price your solution, sell it, and make a profit. If you're not thinking about how your operators will be pricing your product to their customers, you're missing a key component in the value chain.

Sales

Now that you have your distributor strategy, and your initial price is set, it's time to sell. Depending on whether you're selling direct or through a distributor, you will need a sales strategy that fits your method.

Sales, Business Development, and Account Management

One thing that many early companies fail to understand is the difference between sales and business development. Sales is when you have a defined product going into a defined market at a set price. Your salesperson understands the value proposition, and is focused on overcoming objections in the sales process. It's like turning the crank. It's hard work, but it requires little analysis or creativity on the salesperson's part.

Business development is when you don't understand the market yet, and/or you're not 100% clear on the value propositions. I recently spoke to a friend who installed a new VR product in a high-profile location, garnering a ton of mainstream media coverage. She was inundated with product inquiries from around the world. The leads were from malls, airports, entertainment centers, casinos, and on and on. Dozens of market segments were represented. She couldn't keep up with the leads coming in and asked if I could recommend a salesperson.

What I told her was that she needed a business development person, someone who could look at each opportunity and create an evaluation framework to determine if the lead represented a real market opportunity. Often leads can just be noise, and when they're coming in hot and heavy and you don't take the time to go through the framework in this book, it can be overwhelming. This can lead to taking your eye off your primary market, leaving it open for a focused competitor to swoop in and eat your lunch. I've seen it happen often.

One strategy is to have a salesperson focused on your primary target market segments, and a business development person looking at all the other market segments to determine the needs, interest, and opportunities to figure out where to go next. I played this role for a while at Ecast, looking at new markets beyond bars for our digital media platform. We had lots of possibilities, but when I got LG Electronics to invest $5 million in our company to help us bring a digital concierge to their hotel channel, we knew we had found a market opportunity. The salespeople were selling to jukebox operators in bars, but I was out exploring all the other opportunities.

Keeping your sales staff focused is paramount to your success. Figure out early how you will handle this.

Distributors

- If you will be selling to distributors, you will need someone who has good account management skills.

Keeping your sales staff focused is paramount to your success.

Distributors are only as effective as your ability to keep them focused and excited about your product. Don't think you can just sign up a bunch of distributors, sit back, and let the sales roll in. Distributors carry many products, and sometimes even manufacture their own (see Betson's relationship with Raw Thrills as an example in the arcade market).

- Not only will your salesperson be managing your distribution relationships, they will also sell to locations. "How is that?" you ask. Just because a distributor is fulfilling your sales doesn't mean that customers won't call you for product. And that's where the fun starts.

- When a lead comes in, you might be tempted to sell it directly and save the commission you would pay to a distributor. This is called a "house account" and can be a real point of contention for the distributor. Some large customers who can purchase at high volume and negotiate steep discounts because of their scale, leverage, and visibility are legitimate house accounts and distributors will understand. But smaller customers will often try to work direct to save a few bucks. If you want to maintain your distribution relationships, consider letting the distributor fulfill the sale and take the commission. This is something you should discuss with your distributor upon setting up your relationship with them. Ongoing communication is important, and this is why talented account management is at the heart of the salesperson's role.

- Depending on the type, distributors may or may not market your product. Regardless, demand generation is always your responsibility. They will recommend the product to customers who come to them looking for advice (if they actually like and believe in your product, that is). But if you expect them to advertise it, make that explicit in your agreement with them.

> You expect them to advertise it, make that explicit in your agreement with them.

Direct Sales

If you've decided to sell direct, you need a very different type of salesperson. Here they're responsible for managing the sales cycle from cradle to grave. They need to be organized and able to keep track of dozens or even hundreds of prospects simultaneously. They will always be closing, hoping to win the Cadillac and not the steak knives. (If you haven't seen the movie *Glengarry Glen Ross*, put it on your list.) They live for the hunt and the chase, and once the sale is made, they're eager to hand it off to customer service, production, support, or anyone else to free them up to get back to selling.

If you sell direct, you might still need to deal with distribution. If your product is popular, customers might come to their distributor looking for it. And then the distributor will come to you. How to best handle this depends on how you've set up your compensation plans for the sales force.

Regardless of your sales strategy, talk to the distributors in your market. Let them know why you're selling direct, and let them know you're still open to working with them. Keeping the lines of communication open can lead to opportunities down the road.

SECTION 4 –
THE LAUNCH PLAN

NOW THAT YOU'VE got your marketing and positioning done, your target markets selected, some understanding of the customers you will be selling to, and your pricing, distribution, and sales strategy, it's time to get ready for launch. You'll want to plan to make the most effective use of your resources, both financial and human, to get as much leverage as you can. A product launch is like a rocket launch – you need to gain momentum to get off the ground. Your rocket fuel is your people, your creativity, and your

> A product launch is like a rocket launch, you need to gain momentum to get it off the ground.

market knowledge, especially if you're not sitting on a ton of money in the bank.

The first thing you should do at this point is honestly assess your internal capabilities. You're likely to need capabilities in these areas: digital and social marketing, email marketing, web design, event planning, copywriting, graphic design, and public relations, among others. Conduct a gap analysis and see what skills are lurking in your current team, and determine which ones you will need to supplement with contractors or agencies.

We will be looking to create a plan to generate sales leads, market awareness, social proof, third-party validation, and distributor interest. You'll need to formulate a budget for these activities, and depending on where you are in the business lifecycle, these might be things you hand off to agencies with experience, or you might use guerrilla tactics.

I will do my best to summarize the strategies and tactics I've used over the last decade, and most recently with Zero Latency, Hologate, Minority Media, and others.

Crossing the Chasm

To reach any kind of scale in selling your product, one of the first things you will need is social proof and testimonials.

In almost 30 years of selling high-tech solutions to entertainment operators, I've found their psychology follows the model in Geoffrey Moore's *Crossing the Chasm* almost to a T. Start with the innovators or pioneers who will try your product before it's been tested. These people relish being first. My guess is networking is the way you'll find them. They like to brag about their finds, so ask around. Think about how you can help them manage their risk if it doesn't work out for them. They will typically negotiate a deep discount for being first. Make sure that no matter what you do, you get their agreement to get a reference and that you can use their performance results in your promotions.

> Start with the innovators or pioneers who will try your product before it's been tested.

You'll want to move quickly from the pioneers to the early adopters. These are the guys who will jump second; quickly after the pioneers have proven that it works. They need a little bit only of security before they invest. Early adopters know the value of getting in first. They will have something different from their competition. You understand this concept if you've read this far and haven't skipped ahead.

> In order to get the pragmatists, however, be prepared to show numbers and provide references.

It won't take long before pragmatists jump in, because the location-based entertainment business is competitive, and there are generally no barriers to entry. Once someone has a product, everyone else feels the need to add it. It happened with laser tag in the 1990s, and it happened with ropes courses in the 2010s. It happens with everything in trampoline parks, where the rate of innovation is only surpassed by the rate of copying. To get the pragmatists, however, be prepared to show numbers and provide references.

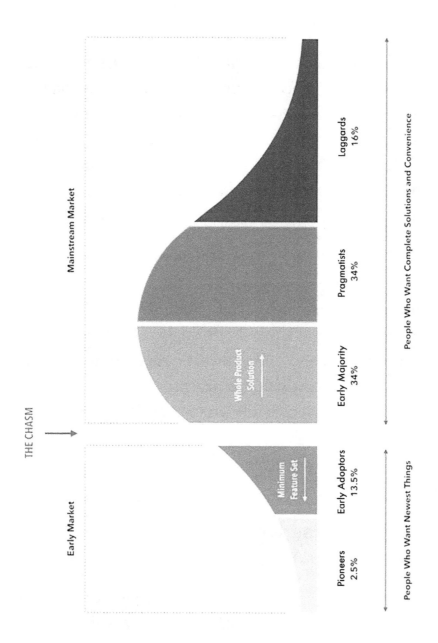

PR

One of the most under-utilized launch strategies is public relations. Not necessarily because companies don't try. Many probably over-invest in this area, hiring expensive agencies who promise the world and underperform. I can't tell you how often I've seen a PR firm send in their big guns to close the account, then put a junior associate just learning the business on the execution plan.

The other mistake I see companies make is thinking that the media care about their product. They just put together a generic product announcement in a press release, and send it to a list of bloggers, trade magazines and websites, and online media outlets. Some will just run what they get sent in a new product release section, but the real coverage they are hoping for never materializes.

> A good PR strategy needs an angle.

This is because a good PR strategy needs an angle. Go back to the positioning work we did earlier and think about WIIFM. What's in it for the writer, the blogger, or the magazine reader? Why should they care? So you've got a new product you're proud of. As do hundreds of other companies. What makes yours news-worthy?

And don't tell me that you're the first. Nobody gives a shit. Seriously. If I had a hundred dollars for everyone who claimed they were the first at something in their marketing and PR messaging, I'd be writing this book on a cruise ship in the Caribbean. Oh wait, I am. Never mind...

Being first only matters to you. Think about it – would you rush to a restaurant that claimed to have invented the first mustard, tomato, and octopus sandwich? Nothing about being first is important in marketing.

Put yourself in the shoes of the news editor at a major website or magazine. They get dozens or even hundreds of press releases every week. What might they be looking for? How might you cut through the noise?

If you want to leverage PR and get a great result, you need to write a story.

If you want to leverage PR and get a great result, you

need to write a story. News editors today, like many people today, are overwhelmed and overworked. They're on a hamster wheel of deadlines trying to generate clicks to drive advertising revenue. You need to serve them up a story on a platter. Don't make them work for it. They won't.

Some media outlets will let you fly them to your office or demo location to trial your product and write a review. In the old days this would have been unheard of, but in today's world it's becoming a widely used practice.

You need to brainstorm your angle. Two years ago, just having a VR product would have got you mainstream media coverage. Now that VR has jumped the shark, you have to work harder.

Sometimes the best angle is human. Few outlets care about your product, so what else is there that could be interesting? What struggles did you overcome to get to launch? What unique stories do you tell your friends when you've had a drink over the weekend?

One of my clients, Jan from Virtuix, has an amazing story. His product, the Omni VR Treadmill, started as a consumer product on Kickstarter. He raised over $1 million, but when it came to fulfill, the shipping costs exceeded the price of the product he sold. Through sheer determination, will, and creativity he came out the other side of that mess and pivoted his company to location-based entertainment. He is now getting ready to launch his second-generation product after having sold over 3000 Omnis in 45 countries. His story will make a great feature in *Inc.* or *Entrepreneur.*

Here are questions to ask yourself that might spur ideas on creating a unique angle for your launch release:

- What made you want to start the business in the first place?

- What struggles have you and your team gone through to get here?

- How will your product change the business or industry?

- What's the background of the founders of your company, and how has that experience led you to this point?

- Have you created new technology? How might this change other industries besides yours?

If your product is truly unique, that might be enough. However, as the market for location-based VR gets crowded, it's becoming harder and harder to differentiate. Taking the time to come up with a unique angle for your PR strategy will pay dividends if you nail it.

Trade Shows
Sponsorships

The good thing about trade shows is that thousands, or even tens of thousands, of your potential customers will be there, hunting for the next big thing. The problem is there are hundreds of other companies showing their version of the next big thing. The goal of pre-show marketing is to increase your odds of capturing the attention of your buyers. It's like insurance for your trade show investment. You've spent a lot of money to get to the show, so if you can spend an extra 10–20% to increase your effectiveness by 200–300%, would you?

> The goal of pre-show marketing is to increase your odds of capturing the attention of your buyers. It's like insurance for your trade show investment.

When doing their first trade show, most companies will invest as much as they can to get the biggest booth they can afford. They put all their budget into the space, booth design and construction, and then have nothing left. This is the equivalent of playing craps; you're rolling the dice that the right people will stumble upon your booth.

At a small trade show, this is a reasonable approach. If you know the show is small enough that everyone will see everything, then the other stuff becomes superfluous. But most people choose bigger shows for their launch, and in those cases, you need to have a pre-show marketing strategy.

In the past several years I've leveraged the use of sponsorships to great success. I used to get sticker shock at the costs (still do, really), but if you have your shit together, you can get great value.

Here are some things you might not think about when it comes to the benefit of a show sponsorship:

Commitment – It's said that everybody wants to be in show business. Companies come and go in the entertainment industry, and operators are sensitive to this notion. If they buy a product from a company that didn't quite make it, they could be stuck with a very expensive doorstop when they need support and service. Sponsoring an event puts your name up there with the big boys, the companies that have been around for a while. This sends a subtle but powerful message that you're in this business for the long haul, and that you value the community and the association.

> Sponsoring an event puts your name up there with the big boys.

Build a list – Many organizations will include in their sponsorship pre- and post-show emails to their members and/or pre-registered attendees. I've found this to be of the highest value, because you can use it to build your own list. No, they won't give you their list – that's generally a violation of every rule of email marketing, and is actually now illegal in the EU, where online rules are becoming more stringent.

What you can do, however, is developed an offer so compelling that recipients of the email from the organization will click over to a landing page you develop specifically for the event. Once there, they have to opt in with their email address to qualify. Here are things you might offer to email recipients.

Free passes to the event – As an exhibitor you typically get several attendee registrations you can offer to customers. You can offer these to the first x-number of opt-in registrations, or randomly pick them from all the opt-ins. Be mindful of sweepstakes rules, or not.

VIP event registration – I will get to the event later in this section, but you can offer a few invites to your special event.

Reserved demo times – Often the most popular attractions will generate long lines at trade shows. With so much to see, the last thing people want is to stand in line for an hour. You can offer a pre-booked time slot so people don't have to wait. Or you can create your own version of Disney's Fast Pass, and have a separate queue so people who registered in advance can jump the line. This latter idea gives attendees the flexibility of coming when it's convenient for them, and removes the hassle of no-shows for you. Or you can combine these two programs and offer both. If they don't show for their scheduled appointment, no worries – just show up in the fast pass line and you're in. This program also sends the message that you expect your attraction to be popular, which is another subtle but powerful marketing message.

Behind-the-scenes sneak peak – Often companies' new products are in development but not ready for prime time. You can offer a sneak-peak demo in a secret location (like a conference room or hotel suite, or even behind a curtain in the booth) to pre-registered attendees. This will also let you weed out competitors who might be doing some good-natured corporate espionage, as you'll have time to vet them before the show.

It's important that you use a landing page for this so you can capture their emails. Your email and landing page need to be designed for high conversion. I won't go into the details of landing page strategy, as there are plenty of resources about this online. I have used Unbounce as a landing page platform with great success, but others work just as well. There are also landing page experts on contracting websites like Upwork, Fivver, and Freelancer. It's worth the few hundred dollars to get an expert involved.

Sponsorships also sometimes come with overhead banners, which can save you thousands of dollars in show contractor fees and banner-printing costs. Hanging a sign over a booth is a good way for people to find you in a huge hall, but it's expensive because you need to hire a cherry picker to reach the rafters. Negotiate this as part of the sponsorship if you can.

Sometimes there's an opportunity to sponsor the show through a targeted segment event. For example, at the IAAPA show in Orlando they have receptions for smaller subcategories of members. They have a water park reception, an FEC reception, and more. Sponsoring these receptions gets you great networking opportunities with your target customers. Sometimes you can show a video to the audience. Sometimes you might get an opportunity to present a keynote presentation. (I'll talk more about speaking opportunities in another section.) You can also hand out your marketing collateral and any swag you might design for the event. (There's more on swag in the promo items chapter.)

I can't overemphasize the power of sponsorship. It gives you immense leverage over your competition. It's an exclusive club, and typically only bigger companies leverage them because of the sticker shock. Sometimes

> I can't overemphasize the power of sponsorship. It gives you immense leverage over your competition.

I wonder if the sponsorship isn't more valuable than the booth itself, but with VR, you really do need to experience it. Sponsorship also gives you access to the association and event organizer. You're essentially *their* VIP customer. If you use this access wisely to build a relationship with the people who run the show, it can pay off for years to come.

Speaking

Most conferences have an education program associated with them. This can be a great way to get your company in front of an audience that takes the business seriously. I find that customers who want to be informed and educated are some of the best clients. They're naturally inquisitive and will listen to what you have to say, as long as you aren't selling to them.

What does that mean? Of course you want to sell to them! That's why you're there, right? Well, yes and no.

There's a time and a place for everything. And the stage is *never* the place from which to sell.

> The stage is *never* the place from which to sell.

Ever been to an Amway meeting at a friend or neighbor's house? That's the closest analogy I can come up with for how it feels to be sitting in an audience expecting to learn, and instead having to watch a sales presentation. Remember when I said nobody gives a shit about your product? How presumptuous is it to think that in a room full of people at a trade show or conference, they all want to hear about your product? There will be plenty of time to sell to those who are interested in other parts of the event.

Instead, use your time on the stage to educate and inform. Don't explain to them how you do stuff. Explain to them why they should care. If you haven't watched Simon Sinek's now-famous Ted Talk 'Start With Why,' now is a good time. In it he talks about how great companies like Apple market effectively by connecting with people around *why* they should care about the product, not what it does or how it does it. My advice is whatever time you have, make it 75% about why, and the rest can be about how and what you do.

If you show the audience respect in this way, they will see you as a trusted authority in whatever it is you're talking about, and they'll seek you out. Then you can engage them in a sales conversation.

Speaking is about building awareness, building your brand, and your thought-leadership position in the industry. It's not for selling.

> Speaking is about building awareness, building your brand, and your thought-leadership position in the industry.

The best conferences recognize this, and will weed out exhibitors from speaking, because they know that most can't resist the urge to sell from the stage. They will instead seek operators with real-world experience to share. If you're an exhibitor, and especially if you're a new member, you will need to convince the education committee that you will not sell from the stage, but instead have something of compelling value you can offer the crowd. This will come in the form of an abstract.

The abstract explains at a summary level what your presentation will cover and, most important, what the audience will take away in knowledge. Having a well-developed abstract is key to nailing down speaking opportunities. It shows the organizer that you're not an amateur (even if you are), and gives them the confidence you won't embarrass them. That's right, those who select speakers are people too, and often their reputation is on the line with who gets on the agenda.

Now there are a few shows out there, especially in the VR industry, that offer pay-to-play speaking opportunities. This means that if you want to speak, you have to purchase the opportunity through some program or sponsorship. At VRLA last year, I sat through a few of these on the main stage. I can say there was barely anyone in the audience for some. I actually felt bad for some presenters, up on stage speaking to 15 people in rooms set for thousands.

I'm not a fan of pay-to-play speaking engagements, but your mileage may vary. If you're going to do it, make sure the organizer will work with you to build an audience.

Often founders like to do keynote presentations because they think that having the stage to themselves is better. However, panel presentations are more engaging, offer more education opportunities for the audience, and are typically less boring. If you're not an experienced speaker, consider getting on a panel. You can even offer to form a panel for the organizer, with you as one of several members. If you're brave you can invite your competitors for a lively discussion. Or you can invite suppliers, or even some of your customers to discuss best practices they've developed around operating your product. If you're already in the market with some test locations, this last idea is gold. You get your customers selling from the stage on your behalf to their peers. There is nothing more powerful.

> Panel presentations are more engaging, offer more education opportunities for the audience, and are typically less boring.

Awards

An often overlooked opportunity at trade shows is the award program. Many shows offer awards for new products, and getting into these programs gives you opportunities that might not be apparent. Foremost, you need to apply early. I can't tell you how many companies just overlook this until the last minute. Often the application deadline is many months before the show itself, which enables the organization to filter through the applications and decide on the entrants most deserving attention at the event.

The application process can be rigorous, but it's critical. Don't rush it, and don't take shortcuts. It's often your application that will enable you to get past the first cut, leading to the opportunity to demo your product to judges on the show floor.

The judges are usually experienced operators who are uniquely qualified to not only judge your product, but also to buy it.

The judges are usually experienced operators uniquely qualified to not only judge your product, but also to buy it. They are also often influencers in the industry and association, so getting in front of them to give a presentation and demo can be worth the cost of going to the show.

If you win an award, the association will generally issue a press release to their constituents about the award winners. You get to issue a press release, too. And you get to brag about it in all your marketing materials for the next year. It's among the most credible social proof you can offer the market, because you can't buy it. I've won Best New Product and Innovator Awards at the major LBE trade shows about 10 times now (I've actually lost count), and I can tell you it's a powerful tool. And it costs you nothing.

Promo Items

Promo items, or SWAG as they're called in the industry, are more times than not a total waste of money. I've heard SWAG stands for Stuff We All Get, but I think it stands for Shit We Acknowledge as Garbage. However,

> I've heard SWAG stands for Stuff We All Get, but I think it stands for Shit We Acknowledge as Garbage.

I have seen rare exceptions to this, when it might have stood for Strategically Worthwhile Appropriate Gold.

The key to making promotional items a worthwhile investment is being on-brand, useful, and novel.

Tim Ruse from Zero Latency went to a military exhibition once and was given a .50cal bullet casing milled into a bottle opener with the exhibiting company's name printed on the side. It was still on his desk a year later, because it was useful and interesting. How many people have a huge shell casing on their desk? And any time he looks at it he knows exactly who it was from.

One of the worst swag ideas ever was the first year I got to Ecast, which was a digital jukebox network. They handed out earplugs. I understand the sentiment as many employees of Ecast were music fans who went to concerts and festivals, where earplugs can be a welcome relief. But for their audience, it was a weird giveaway because it suggested that you might not want to actually listen to the music they were delivering. It was like handing out blindfolds at a movie theater.

At Zero Latency's global launch at IAAPA in 2016, I came up with the idea of handing out custom-printed Google

Cardboard VR viewers as swag at the show. I thought it was a good way to stay on-brand, but also educate people about VR. It was still early days and most people had not done VR. Zero Latency created a VR-friendly promo video and we gave away hundreds of them. It was on-brand and novel, but it wasn't useful. It turned out to be confusing. People who had never done VR thought it was cool, but then many would ask, "Is this your product?" I was horrified that people could confuse a $2 giveaway with a $600,000 immersive VR platform. It was a waste of money and effort, and might have done more damage than good.

The next year, Andre Lawless came up with the Zombie Stress Doll, which was a huge hit. Zero Latency was releasing a new game called Outbreak Origins, a 30-minute zombie adventure. The zombie stress doll was on-brand, cool, and useful. It's still on the desk of lots of people.

Coming up with good swag is a challenge. My advice is that if you can't come up with something that is on-brand, useful, and unique, your money is better spent elsewhere.

Uniforms

Something that is often overlooked at trade shows is the opportunity that your employees present when walking the miles and miles they will cover during the event. Their time at the show, from the moment they leave their hotel room to the moment they go to bed, is an outdoor advertising opportunity.

From just a simple logo t-shirt to a coordinated outfit, 90% of companies miss this cheap opportunity. When I launched X-Men Laser Tag at IAAPA in 1997, where we won the Best Booth award, we had our employees wearing jumpsuits with the X-Men logo emblazoned on them. We found them in an industrial supply catalog, and took them to a local screen printer. The sales staff wore blue sport coats with an embroidered patch on the chest that said, "Xavier's School For Gifted Children," which was the name of the institute at which the X-Men lived and trained. It was professional and on-brand, and people were actually talking about it at the show.

One of the other more cheeky uniforms we had at a show was at Ecast at the height of our competition with TouchTunes. We created a campaign called Follow the

Leader, which was a poke at our competition for consistently copying our product features. We purchased bowling shirts and had Follow the Leader printed on the back, which was a message to anyone walking behind us that we were the industry leader.

> **Think of your uniform as a billboard opportunity.**

Think of your uniform as a billboard opportunity. What do you want it to say to people standing in front of you, and what message do you want to say to those standing behind you? If you think about the media opportunity of a t-shirt on a cost-per-impression basis compared to all the other things you will be spending money on, you will understand that it can quickly become your most cost-effective advertisement.

Special Events

A VIP event is a great choice for getting you in front of your key prospects to allow you to deliver a focused and intentional message without the distractions of the show floor. It can be expensive, but on a cost-per-attendee basis, it can be effective.

Expect to spend between $50 and $100 per attendee. That means if you cap it at 100 people, it could cost you $5–10K. That might sound like a lot, but when you look at companies that spend $100K to be at a show, who might walk away with a couple hundred leads they spend 5 minutes each with, the value of spending an hour or more with a group of highly qualified prospects can be a good use of your marketing budget.

Typically a VIP event will comprise three components: a welcome reception or happy hour with a bar, a formal presentation with Q and A, and some food and entertainment.

> The value of spending an hour or more with a group of highly qualified prospects can be a really good use of your marketing budget.

My experience has been that starting with a limited bar (one or two drinks max) to relax people is a good start. Then move into a more formal presentation. Again, this is an opportunity to educate your audience; be wary of doing too much selling. Introduce them to key members of your staff, which can personalize your company to them. Tell them a story about why you came up with the product you're featuring. Show them a video of the product and share with them high-level features and benefits, but keep this part short.

The best content will come from questions posed by the audience. They're there because they're curious, so get them asking questions. Also, have someone from your team writing down the questions they ask, because after the show you will do an audit of your marketing materials. This is to ensure that all the questions they were asking are answered in your collateral.

After the presentation, invite them to mingle. Depending on the time of day or night, you might offer food now. If you have the event at a place with entertainment, you can offer drink tickets for them to stay, enjoy themselves, and mingle with your staff and their peers.

If your product can be demonstrated at the event, this is a great opportunity to showcase your product offering in a more personal way, and also to show some of the behind-the-scenes products in development to make your VIPs feel special.

I find having the VIP event on the second night of a three- or four-day show is the best window, but check with the event organizer to see what other events are happening. Sometimes the hardest thing is to find a window where you're not competing with bigger or more well-known events. You will want to promote the event in advance via all of your digital marketing means, driven through the landing page so you can build your list. You can also print out 150 formal invitations, put them in nice envelopes and ask people to drop by the booth to pick up their invite. You can also hand out invites to people you meet during the show who you feel you want to spend some extra time with.

Invite distributors early, and allow them to invite their best customers. You can also invite key members of the trade press, and even the show organizers as a gesture of goodwill, though most will politely decline because they're too busy.

> Make sure to invite distributors early, and offer them the opportunity to invite their best customers.

You can also run a VIP event at a show or event where you aren't exhibiting. Anywhere your customers might be gathering is an opportunity for an event. Hologate held a joint VIP event with a co-working space in LA during the VRLA conference that attracted hundreds of people. The formula above is just one of many. Get creative.

Collateral

Most people tend to overthink their collateral for a trade show. My personal experience is that I walk around collecting brochures that wind up stacked in the corner of my office for two years until I get around to cleaning, then I dump them in the garbage. Is that just me?

Trade show collateral needs to walk the fine line between being small and light enough to be easily carried around, and large enough to stand out and get your desired message across.

> If you went into a car dealer to buy a Toyota or a Ferrari, what would you expect the brochure to be like in each case?

The price range of your product and solution will factor in. If you're selling a $20K game you can get away with a standard catalog or cut sheet, which is a two-sided, full-color, letter-size flyer. If you're selling a six-figure product, expand it to multiple pages. If you went into a car dealer to buy a Toyota or a Ferrari, what would you expect the brochure to be like in each case?

A word about volume printing. I always get asked the question, "How many should I print?" I've usually found that printing enough for 5% of the expected attendees is sufficient, but the worst thing imaginable is running out. The cost of printing extras is marginal. Balance this with the knowledge that the brochure will likely be obsolete after the show, and many companies just leave the extras on the show floor to be thrown away.

Booth Design

Booth design could be a whole book in itself. It's highly dependent on your budget, the size of your space, and your product. Having built hundreds of booths in my career, there are some things I've learned that I believe are universal.

One of the biggest mistakes I consistently make in my booth designs is to overlook logo size and placement. More times than I care to remember I've stood back after a couple of days of exhausting booth-building to reflect on my creation, only to face-palm myself and scream, "Where the fuck is the logo?!" Sure, it's there in little places, but I often miss the big branding opportunity to place the logo front and center. Often we get so caught up in the product message we forget that the company brand is just as important. Don't forget the logo.

Pay for the extra carpet padding. Your employees will thank you after two long days on their feet.

Pay for the extra carpet padding. Your employees will thank you after a couple of long days on their feet.

Your customers are tired. They've been walking for days. Give them a comfortable place to sit and hang out. For the last decade, my focus in trade show design has been on creating welcoming and comfortable opportunities to sit and talk. At IAAPA for the last two years I purchased a giant red U-shaped couch that was the centerpiece of the booth. I accommodated the entire team of 6 from Dave & Buster's, who commented that they appreciated the opportunity to sit down and rest.

Set up a way for your customers to connect with prospects. It might be too early if you're just launching, but if a few customers have trialed your product and like it, how might you create an environment for prospects to interact with them? At Ecast we created the Download Lounge, which was a giant VIP lounge behind a 14-foot-high curtain. To get in you needed a VIP lanyard. We gave our customers one color and our invited prospects another so they could seek each other out. We ran that booth for several years it was so successful. You can use this idea at your VIP event, too.

Don't rely on WiFi for demos.

Don't rely on WiFi for demos. If your product requires a WiFi connection to work, and you plan to do demonstrations, you might want to either bring a senior network engineer with you for set-up, or consider another option. There is so much WiFi interference at a big trade show that it's more likely you'll struggle to get your product working. Zero Latency had to hard-wire their gun controllers to their backpacks in 2015 to get their demo to work, and had to limit it to one player at a time. We wound up setting up a location off site, and shuttling people back and forth during the show. VR Studios spent the majority of their four days at IAAPA in 2017 trying to get their platform working. WiFi is a killer.

Renting equipment at trade shows is one of the most financially painful aspects of marketing. When you rent a TV for more than it costs to buy at Costco, you realize that trade shows are a for-profit business. In 2016 I had finally had enough. I decided not to rent anything. I got to the show early and purchased everything I needed at IKEA, Costco, and Pier 1.

When the show was over, I found a charity that helps homeless families establish themselves in homes again. I donated the entire set-up: couch, tables, chairs, rugs, pillows, TV, entertainment center, lamps, and more. It saved a few dollars, was way more work, but was truly rewarding. I encourage you to do the same.

Site Openings

A new site opening or product installation is a good opportunity for a launch event. This is especially true if you're a component manufacturer, or you make a product or software that becomes part of a larger solution.

As opposed to a trade show, where the date is fixed, a site opening can and often moves its date. There are so many factors that go into opening a retail location – zoning, inspections, weather, supply chain, etc. – that it can be unpredictable. If you're using a third-party opening as a launch event, flexibility is key.

> A new site opening or product installation is a good opportunity for a launch event.

While you may be part of the press release for the site, you will want to create your own press release and strategy to leverage the noise that the higher profile release might generate. A great recent example of this was VR Studios and the Jurassic World VR attraction at Dave & Buster's.

Jurassic World VR is a four-player motion simulator where players don headsets and use controllers to "tag" dinosaurs to save them. The software was developed by The Virtual Reality Company, the motion-based hardware was from Talon Systems, the IP was licensed by Universal, HTC provided the HMDs and controllers, and VR Studios developed the operating system. The main PR around this product was a joint release by VRC and Dave & Buster's. HTC had their own release, too. But VR Studios played this masterfully, issuing their press release a moment after VRC and Dave & Buster's did. When news hit the wire, editors and writers doing any search on Google came across the VR Studios release and included them in the story. They garnered a ton of press they would not have gotten had they relied on a brief mention in the original Dave & Buster's release.

> You can also have a VIP event around a site opening.

You can also have a VIP event around a site opening, so you can invite your prospects, media, partners, etc. This will just add to the sense of excitement for the overall event. Bringing in an entertainer can add to the allure, and you can share the cost between multiple parties if they're all on board.

Getting in the habit of announcing your site openings, especially in the early days, will give you a steady supply of awareness in the marketplace. And your customers will love the attention, because it adds to their market awareness, too. Everybody loves to read their name in the paper.

You'll need a strategy to make sure your role in the overall launch is clear, without taking away from the site-opening story. This can require some nuance, but by carefully coordinating with the site owner, it can be done. As with all things, communication is key.

Email Marketing

Email is the cornerstone of any digital marketing effort. Building your email list should be a focus of your entire marketing plan. When someone gives you their email address, they're giving you permission to communicate with them. Please don't underestimate the gravity of this permission.

The rules around building, maintaining, and using an email list continue to get more and more stringent. The recent EU rulings around General Data Protection Regulation (GDPR) have increased the penalties asso-

> Building your email list should be a focus of your entire marketing plan.

ciated with the abuse of email for companies around the world. You must pay attention to these continuously evolving regulations.

I've talked about using event sponsorships and landing pages to build an email list. All of your social media and content marketing strategies should ultimately drive traffic to high-converting landing pages that add to your list.

There are plenty of email marketing gurus out there you can follow. I've paid Vanessa Cabrera (www.vanes-sa-cabrera.com) for coaching, and have subscribed to and follow the List Grow program from Mike Dillard. This is another area where online expertise is widely available on platforms like Upwork, Freelancer, and Fiverr. Getting your email strategy right is critical to the long-term success of your company. Don't skimp on this one.

> When you build a list, use it sparingly. Try to be respectful of the permission you've been given.

When you build a list, use it sparingly. Use it to educate and inform. Try to be respectful of the permission you've been given. Think about what you might want someone to send you. It's that simple.

One word about buying lists – don't. Any list that's for sale is generally not worth the bits it's made from, and the minute you email anyone on the list you're violating several laws. I've had random people offer to sell me lists of amusement buyers, IAAPA members, and other groups. Sometimes I've had them send me a sample list. Out of 1000 names there might be 20 in the purported market they were claiming – and those were probably bad emails, anyway. You will get high bounce rates, high unsubscribe rates, and high spam-reporting rates, all of which will affect your ability to send email in the future. The worst thing that can happen is you're blacklisted by major ISPs, and then even your legitimate emails get sent to spam folders. Getting this reversed can be impossible without changing your email domain, which is a massive pain in the ass. So just don't.

Landing Pages

I've mentioned landing pages in other sections, and for those who are unfamiliar with the basics, I'll explain. A landing page differs from your website. A website is a multi-use platform. It's used to inform people, give them a way to contact you, to offer support, maybe build community. It's kind of like a Swiss Army knife.

A landing page is more like a scalpel. It's designed to do one thing really well. And that's convert a browser (the person, not the application) into a transaction.

A website is like a swiss army knife. A landing page is more like a scalpel.

That transaction can be almost anything, but usually in this context I'm talking about giving you an email address and permission to communicate.

To gain this permission, you need to offer something of value. A sales pitch is not of value to a prospect, it's of value to you. Remember WIIFM from the prospects perspective. What are you offering of value that will get them to hand over their highly valued email address?

It could be a white paper, a case study, an invitation to an event, a discount, membership in a community, or any number of things. The more value, the higher the conversion.

One of the unique aspects of a landing page is that once you get on it, the only way off is to make the transaction or close the window. There is no menu to browse or other pages to link to. It's a captive page where there are two choices – transact or leave.

Landing page development is hard science. It's not art. There are best practices around page layout, word counts, even button colors. You can study all this online or hire an expert. I advise hiring an expert, plentiful on places like Upwork, Freelancer, and Fiverr. You can also watch training videos and webinars on Unbounce, ClickFunnels, and other platforms that specialize in helping you build landing pages.

Associations

Philosopher Abraham Maslow said that a sense of belonging is a base human need. We all want to be a member of a tribe. It's part of what drives human behavior. An association is just another form of tribe, where all the members have their business or industry in common.

Associations often solicit supplier memberships with discounts to trade shows, as that's the most obvious means of creating a return on investment for annual dues. They recognize that suppliers are just looking to sell to their members, and rules that dictate the terms of engagement. Many companies stop at that level of involvement, which is a shame, because they're missing out on a much richer opportunity.

> Getting involved in one of these committees not only shows you're serious about the industry.

Every association has committees comprised of members. These committees help run things like events, membership drives, government lobbying, foreign business development, industry promotion, and more. Getting involved in committees not only shows you're serious about the industry, but will also help you network with others who are serious. It instantly puts you on the inside. Associations are built on volunteers and they are usually desperate to activate their membership in this way.

Almost every market segment you might target has their own association. While IAAPA is huge and it's easy to get lost, there are associations for trampoline parks, skating rinks, zoos, museums, bowling centers, family entertainment centers, and more. Get involved in the association that represents your target market segment. They will welcome your involvement and your target customers will respect your efforts. You will learn more than you can imagine, which will make you a better supplier and a more valued member of the community.

Content Marketing
Case Studies

A great way to get your success stories out there is by writing or commissioning a case study or white paper. A case study on a customer who has successfully implemented your product or solution offers fantastic third-party validation, and can cement your relationship with that customer. A case study is a joint effort between you and the customer. The customer should be contributing much of the content, even if you or a third party is writing it. You don't want it to be a sales pitch in the way you would be selling the product. It should be more like a third-party referral sale, where a friend tells you about something they're excited about, like a new restaurant in town, and you immediately decide you want to try it.

If you don't quite have a success story yet, a white paper is another great way to get your name out there. A white paper is designed to educate and inform, not sell. It's all about creating fertile background information that sets the reader up to understand why your product solves a problem. You will spend most of the time writing about the problem.

> It's all about creating fertile background information that sets the reader up to understand why your product is a perfect solution to a problem.

I wrote a white paper in 2016 about why the consumer market for VR would not happen. Zero Latency "sponsored" it and we used it as the hub of our content marketing strategy. People could download it for free, in exchange for an opt-in email address. You can download my most recent white paper here as a template (and see an example of a landing page in the process): www.bobcooney.com/innovate

I wrote the white paper to specifically combat the most common and challenging objections I was getting from the market. Customers were concerned that everyone would soon have VR in their homes, and that an investment in location-based VR would soon become obsolete. They were worried that the same thing that happened with video games in the 1990s would happen with VR, but faster. So the white paper not only set me up as an authority on the market so everything I said was more credible, it also overcame the number-one objection that Zero Latency was getting room sales prospects.

Social Media

Business-to-business social media these days is all about LinkedIn. While there are some good Facebook groups around, Facebook makes it difficult to target these groups with ads. It's difficult to target your audience on Facebook, Instagram, Snapchat, and other consumer social platforms.

LinkedIn has really upped their game in the last year with targeted ad opportunities. They can seem expensive compared to other social platforms, but the business nature of the audience warrants the higher cost. Their Sponsored Content campaigns have been good value for some of my clients. You pay per impression and they make sure your content shows up in the streams of your target audience.

Any effective social media campaign requires content that the audience will be interested in. Again, it can't just be a sales pitch. When was the last time you opted-in to be sold something intentionally? Nobody wants to be contacted by a salesperson.

> **Add to the conversation. Answer questions for people. Become a trusted expert.**

If you've developed a white paper, case study, webinar, or other informative and educational content, LinkedIn is a great place to build your audience. Also, be part of the groups on all the social platforms focused on your market. Add to the conversation. Answer questions for people. Become a trusted expert. But don't sell in the group because you risk being banned. All groups have rules of engagement, so pay attention and respect them.

User Groups

Another popular form of social media is Facebook, which I love for creating user groups. By creating a private group and inviting your customers, you have a forum to educate and inform, and to nurture a community around your product. In the group you can engage both customers and prospects. As I've mentioned before, having customers talk about your product to prospects can be a super-powerful thing.

Many companies fear putting their prospects with their customers, because of what their customers might say. My experience with this is that if you make an effort to make your customers happy, this is never a problem. Your customers need you to succeed. If you fail, they're stuck with an irrelevant and possibly unsupported product.

If you put your trust in them, they will recognize this and do the right thing. There are always exceptions – those customers who are just angry or can never be made happy. One thing I've found is that the community usually controls these loud voices. If they're being unreasonable, other customers will call them out on it.

You will also gain tremendous insight into how your customers are using your product, and how they view your company. You will have an open channel for dialogue, which will create a true community of dedicated customers. I wish I could get more companies to do this, but their fear usually gets in the way. I encourage you to try it. If it blows up you can always shut it down, but my guess is that you will thank me.

If you create your own user group, I advise you to use a private group on Facebook. I know people who have tried to do this on other platforms, such as LinkedIn or Slack, and they complain about a lack of engagement. Regardless of what you think about Facebook, there are over 3 billion people on it, with most engaging every day; some every hour. Someone once said to catch a fish, go where the fish are. I don't know who that was, or if anyone actually said that before I just wrote it, but it's true. All these fish are on Facebook. You can control access with a private group, so only people you invite or approve get in. It's not perfect, but it works.

Webinars

I love webinars. They're like mini keynote presentations. Not everyone wants to read a white paper or a case study, so a webinar is a great way to reach those who want a more lively and interactive way of receiving your information.

Webinars are super easy to set up and run. There are some great platforms out there. Many people use Zoom, which is also a great video-conferencing platform. Others use GoToWebinar, which is part of GoToMeeting, another video-conferencing solution. I use a platform called Demio because it's new and has specific features I find compelling. It's super easy to use; you can set up a webinar in less than 5 minutes. When I tried some of the other platforms, it felt like I needed to take a class just to set them up. And during the webinar I was so busy trying to manage settings and communicating with viewers on chat that I was constantly distracted. Demio simplifies things so you can just concentrate on your message. If you use the link at www.bobcooney.com/resources to sign up you will save $25, and I get a referral fee.

But it doesn't matter which platform you use, because they all do the same basic thing: allow you to broadcast your presentation to a bunch of people at once, and let them interact with you via chat, or you can even bring them on screen with video.

As opposed to other digital content marketing strategies that are asynchronous (you put your content out there and people consume it when they want), webinars are held at a certain time. The best part of a webinar comes from the interaction with and between your attendees. This means they all need to be there at the same time.

Many webinar platforms have replay functionality for those who didn't get to view it in real time. Some, like Demio, offer a "like-live replay," which makes it seem like it's live even if it's recorded. They do this by recreating the chat stream for each new viewer and giving them a chance to add to the chat.

> **Reach out in advance to registered attendees and ask them for specific questions they may have about the subject of the webinar.**

I try to keep my webinars to about 30 or 40 minutes of programmed content, and then leave it open-ended for questions. When I promote a webinar about a week or two beforehand, I like to contact registered attendees and ask them for specific questions they have about the subject of the webinar. This gives me time to research their questions if I don't know the answers, contact other experts, and then deliver content that's meaningful to them and other audience members. It's like user generated content and shows that I am in tune with their needs.

Springboard VR has done a great job of holding monthly webinars. Getting on a schedule and building frequency will force you to create content and help position your company as a thought leader in the industry. This builds trust and ultimately makes it easier for people to buy from you.

Don't get caught up in your webinar content not being good enough. If you contact the audience in advance like I do, your content will be awesome, and people will love it.

Blogging

Blogging is often the foundation of any content marketing strategy. It can also prove to be the most challenging. I can't tell you how many websites I see with a half-dozen blog posts, each one about a week apart, and then nothing (even mine).

Companies have the best of intentions when it comes to blogging. But where they fail is making it someone's job. Someone needs to get up every morning thinking, "What am I going to blog about today?" Or better yet, know they need to look at their editorial calendar, where the answer will be right there for them (more on page 197).

I don't recommend farming out blogging to a third party, even though some people have had success with this. If you want your content to resonate with your audience, ideally you want it to be unique and relevant. It might be hard for someone outside your business and industry to pull this off.

If you want to blog daily, there's no shortage of stuff you can write about. If you're subscribing to industry newsletters, or Google news alerts, you will have something to write about every day. Just make sure it's relevant to your audience.

Consistency is critical with blogging. It can be once a day, once a week, or twice a month, but get on a schedule and stick to it. Peter Cook, one of the founders of the Thought Leaders Business School I attend in Australia, says that it's better to just get it out than to make it perfect. Blogging is an informal means of communication. Don't be sloppy, but don't strive for perfection. Strive for consistency.

Blogging is like saving for retirement. If you invest consistently, people will subscribe to your blog. This becomes a part of your email list and is like money in the bank. At some point a percentage of your subscribers will convert. You just don't know when.

> **Blogging is like saving for retirement. If you invest consistently, people will subscribe.**

Video Channels

Video is exploding as a means of content marketing. The popularity of streaming video sites like Twitch, YouTube, and Facebook Live has brought the tools for video production and delivery to every mobile phone. You can stream video anytime, anywhere there's a connection.

There are some best practices emerging on video production due to the nature of how people consume video now. One you might have noticed is subtitles. Putting a video out without subtitles assumes that people are where they can listen to the audio. Since most video is now consumed on mobile devices, often in public, you cannot assume audio is enabled. Many browsers now disable audio on auto-start videos, forcing the viewer to activate the volume bar.

> Putting a video out without subtitles assumes that people are in a situation where they can listen to the audio.

There are many ways to get your audio transcribed into subtitles. YouTube even has a built-in transcription feature. There are third-party platforms out there that do it as well (check out www.rev.com). Plus, sites like Fiverr are full of people who will take your transcription and add nice-looking subtitles to the video for a few dollars. It's money well spent.

You will want to build a YouTube channel (and maybe Vimeo, too) to host all your videos. Here you can have product videos, webinar replays, and educational videos, all in one place. YouTube does a great job of SEO too, so the more content you have, the more they will bring you to the top of a Google search.

I'm a big fan of Facebook Live. It's casual, fun, and easy. You can use third-party tools to download the videos, add subtitles, then upload them to your YouTube channel for later consumption. It's a great way to build community, and Facebook prioritizes Live videos on people's streams, so you're more likely to build your audience.

Another place to spend a few bucks is on an intro and outro. This is usually a motion graphic that brands the beginning and end of your videos. It's also called a bumper. You can get them cheap on Fiverr.

Just remember, like blogging, it's better to just get it out there than to make it perfect. Consistency is key. Have fun with it, and you'll see the payoff.

Editorial Calendar

The editorial calendar is a tool that marketing organizations use to track and plan their marketing initiatives. Having everything in a calendar can help coordinate between content marketing, press releases, and the editorial content of media publications and platforms.

If you've never done one before I recommend starting with a monthly view. Keep it simple at first. I like to use a big wall calendar, but you can use a spreadsheet if that's your thing. At the top, have a column for each month. On the left, a row for each type of communication channel. It can get super granular at some point, but start off broad.

At the top I would have a column for each trade publication. Most will publish an editorial calendar of their own. Many magazines have a feature subject each month. Most will be irrelevant to you, but if they're having a VR issue, or an issue on your target segment, you want to know that well in advance.

These featured issues present guideposts for your content marketing. If the industry is talking about something that month, you can use that zeitgeist to drive your stories, as long as you can find a relevant thread.

Below the trades you can have rows for press releases, social media, blogs, videos, webinars, case studies, white papers, and any other content you're generating.

Having a specific theme each month can make it easier on those you task with generating content. Keeping it consistent during the month will make it more likely to reach your audience. When your social posts support the message in your webinar, which supports the news you're putting out via a press release, which is all supported by your paid advertising in a trade publication also running stories about your industry segment, people get it.

Besides the editorial calendar, an event calendar can help you decide what events to attend and in what fashion. If you have a new product release on your editorial calendar, you might target a launch at an event the same month. Or maybe you intend to have a

> Having a specific theme each month can make it easier on those you task with generating content.

new webinar in July, and there's a conference in August where you could offer it as a keynote. Too often we learn of event opportunities too late to effectively act on them. We make last-minute decisions and scramble, distracting our entire organization and actually getting little in the way of results.

It takes about a day for an intern to research all of the events in VR, LBE, and your chosen segments. Every month, your team should review the event and editorial calendar and make conscious decisions about what you will do. Plan a year in advance, update quarterly, and review monthly so everyone is on the same page.

Trade Media

Every trade has its media platforms. In the old days these were restricted to magazines, or rags as they were known. Now they've been supplemented or even replaced by websites, online newsletters, and other digital platforms.

There are broad trade media platforms and niche ones. You will want to figure out what yours looks like early. At the highest level you have the horizontal sites that cover VR, digital entertainment, gaming, etc. Sites like Upload and Road to VR cover virtual reality almost exclusively. You have gaming sites like Polygon. You have magazines like *Hollywood Reporter* that cover movie-based digital interactive content stories. You have niche market magazines like *Replay*, which covers amusement games for FECs, and *Funworld* that covers amusement parks.

You will want to create and manage a media list, which will take some research initially, but will become a valuable resource. Discover who the publisher and editor are. Look for stories on your competition and find out who the author is. Keep track of them. Reach out and let them know you like

> Build relationships with your trade media.

their work (but only if you do – don't bullshit them, they will know). Build relationships with your trade media.

I build such solid relationships with the editors of the major trade journals in my industry that at trade shows we get together and have a smoker once a year. I was the only non-media member of the group. We would discuss the industry, trends, developments, tell stories, and smoke cigars. They became a trusted group of friends.

One day I picked up a contract with a company called PayRange, which has a mobile payment platform for vending machines. I knew next to nothing about the vending business, other than sometimes I lose my money trying to buy a Snickers bar. So I contacted my friend Nick Montano, long-time editor of *Vending Times*. He agreed to walk me around the NAMA vending show and teach me. I got a two-hour masterclass on the history of vending.

It didn't hurt that in every company I worked, I advertised with the trade journals. Support your trade publications with your ad dollars, and nurture the relationships. Even if you don't see the ROI in month one, a concerted and consistent presence will not only yield results in advertising, but you'll also find your news is covered with a higher profile and more consistency.

Unlike mainstream media, where they get more news releases than they could ever publish, trade media is generally hungry for news. Nick explained that his job was to promote the trade. He always tried to find a balance between news, insights, and industry promotion.

New company profiles are welcome. News releases too. You can even submit a draft yourself and they'll edit it. I write regularly for *RePlay Magazine*, who are actively looking to cover new companies and new products. You can send an email to the editor, Key Snodgress, at editor@replaymag.com right now and tell her your story. Let her know Bob sent you. Who knows, I might follow up and offer to write a feature.

CLOSING

I HOPE SOME of the information in this book is useful to you. If you've read this far, and you're not skipping to the end to discover whodunnit, then maybe it is. I invite you to use what works for you. There is no right or wrong way. The history books are littered with stories of entrepreneurs who said "Fuck YOU!" They did things the "wrong way" and made billions of dollars in the process.

If you need help at some point, here are some resources for you.

I run a Facebook mentoring group that is free and open to anyone who can contribute. There is an amazing community there of people who might have already solved the problem you're facing. Ask them for help. You can join on my website at www.bobcooney.com/mentoring or search Facebook for Bob Cooney's Location Based VR Mentoring Group.

You can download the templates I use, like Empathy and Expectation Maps, Segmentation Workbooks, SWOT Analysis, etc. on my website: www.bobcooney.com/tools

I run occasional workshops on this material, so stay tuned at www.bobcooney.com/events

I can help you run this program inside your company, either over a 13-week mentoring program, or as an intensive two-day workshop. Email me at vrbob@bob-cooney.com for more info.

My next book with be *Real Money from Virtual Reality – Operator's Edition*, which will be a deep dive into how to select the best VR attraction for your location, along with tips, tricks, and best practices for operating, marketing, and maximizing your investment in VR. Coming spring 2019. Thank you for your time, and I wish you the best of luck in your journey.

Bob

www.ingramcontent.com/pod-product-compliance
Lightning Source LLC
Chambersburg PA
CBHW071117050326
40690CB00008B/1254